The Left-Handed Story

WRITERS ON WRITING
Jay Parini, Series Editor

A good writer is first a good reader. Looking at craft from the inside, with an intimate knowledge of its range and possibilities, writers also make some of our most insightful critics. With this series we will bring together the work of some of our finest writers on the subject they know best, discussing their own work and that of others, as well as concentrating on craft and other aspects of the writer's world.

Poet, novelist, biographer, and critic, Jay Parini is the author of numerous books, including *The Apprentice Lover* and *One Matchless Time: A Life of William Faulkner*. Currently he is D. E. Axinn Professor of English & Creative Writing at Middlebury College.

The Left-Handed Story

Writing and the Writer's Life

Nancy Willard

The University of Michigan Press

Ann Arbor

2011 2010 2009 2008   4 3 2 1

A CIP catalog record for this book is available from the British Library.

Library of Congress Cataloging-in-Publication Data

Willard, Nancy.
    The left-handed story : writing and the writing life / by Nancy
Willard.
        p.   cm.
    ISBN-13: 978-0-472-09999-3 (cloth : alk. paper)
    ISBN-10: 0-472-09999-X (cloth : alk. paper)
    ISBN-13: 978-0-472-06999-6 (pbk. : alk. paper)
    ISBN-10: 0-472-06999-3 (pbk. : alk. paper)
    1. Willard, Nancy.   2. Authorship.   I. Title.

PS3573.I444Z46   2008
818'.5409—dc22   2007030969

*for Kathy Bean
and William Gosling*

Contents

Preface

Write from what you know, our first writing teachers told us.

So in this book I tell stories of failures survived, dilemmas solved, books finished, editors that helped me, and writers whose work I love that inspired me. I go back to my own experience as a writer. But all writers know that the source of their work runs deeper than literary influences. Our writing teachers let us find out for ourselves what they really meant: write about any time or place or person you can imagine your way into—write from more than you know.

The essays in this book include family stories, told and retold. The book I write today has put down its roots in my earliest memories long before I know I want to write it. The kind of memories that give us stories and break our hearts do not come like obedient hounds when we call them. No, memories choose the writer, not the other way around.

Writers learn a great about their craft from books but they learn more, I think, from listening to ordinary speech and what it can tell us about each other and ourselves. *The Left-Handed Story* includes some of the lectures I've given at various places, but it also includes essays on teaching, on ancestors and rural life, and two interviews, neither of them with writers.

The Writer's Craft

"What We Write about
When We Write about Love"

⟨∞⟩

THE FIRST BOOK I EVER wanted to steal was a slim blue paperback called *Stories of Love and Passion*. It showed a woman in a low-cut gown and elbow-length gloves eyeing a man with a goatee and moustache: the devil, I supposed, or one of his minions. Because the devil wore a striped polo shirt and a beret, I assumed he was on vacation—a cruise, perhaps. The woman was giving him a sly smile; she had one arm raised, as if she were waving at someone just out of the picture.

I was twelve, going on sixteen. Every summer my mother and sister and I moved from Ann Arbor, Michigan, to a ramshackle cottage sixty miles away, in the sleepy settlement of Stoney Lake. My father, who was teaching summer school, drove to Stoney Lake every Friday after his last class, and on Sunday he drove the family car back to Ann Arbor.

All week long the old men of Stoney Lake went fishing and the young men went to work in town or at the gravel pit across the lake, and the mothers and grandmothers sat on their front porches and watched the dust rise and fall in the dirt road, and gossiped in Italian, and so the air hung heavy with their secrets. Only our house felt as dull as a convent.

Thank God for my mother's younger sister, Nell, who chose to spend the first month of her summer vacation with us and whose *Stories of Love and Passion* showed me what I was missing. She kept the book on the nightstand, next to her Madame DuBarry Beauty

Box. Her favorite story, "Room Eleven," was no secret; when I picked up that slim blue volume, it obligingly opened to page 33:

> She picked all her lovers from the army and kept them three years. The time of their sojourn in the garrison. In short, she not only had sense. . . . She gave the preference to men of calm allurement, like herself, but they must be handsome. She also wished them to have had no previous entanglements, any passion having the power to leave traces, or that had made any trouble. Because the man whose loves are mentioned is never a very discreet man.
>
> After having decided upon the one she would love for the three years of his regulation sojourn, it only remained to throw down the gauntlet.[1]

Not for her second-graders at Northville Elementary did Nell pluck her eyebrows, oil her eyelashes, and rouge her cheeks. She was young, pretty, and twice divorced. When she scanned the *Oxford Weekly,* she was appalled to find that God hosted all the regular social events announced in its pages; even square dancing was held in the basement of the Methodist church. The only gatherings that escaped His watchful eye were auctions.

The auctions always took place on somebody's front lawn. One hot Sunday in July, we stood opposite the high school, listening to the auctioneer's patter and laughing at his jokes.

Nell bid on whatever looked like a bargain. Who knows why we suddenly want what we don't need? When an upright piano was pushed into view and the auctioneer shouted, "What am I bid for this piano?" my mother bid ten dollars.

"Ten dollars!" sneered the auctioneer. "Madame, I'd buy it myself for ten dollars if I had a place to put it. Look at the carving on this thing."

"Do it play?" called a voice from the back of the crowd.

"Play? Play?" The auctioneer touched middle C. "Can anyone here give a demonstration?"

Nell was on the platform in an instant. She pulled up a kitchen chair, she played "You Are My Sunshine" and "Four-Leaf

Clover," then eased into the rippling improvisation she used to quiet her second graders.

"Twenty!" shouted a voice in the back.

"Twenty-five!" shouted my mother.

"Twenty-five going once, twenty-five going twice—"

The auctioneer paused. The silence was deafening.

"All done at twenty-five!"

"My God," whispered Mother, "where will we put a piano?"

While the auctioneer's assistant was smoothing Mother's five-dollar bills and tucking them into the cashbox, Nell was talking to one of the movers, a man whose sweat-soaked shirt stuck to his back in ragged patches. He was the only mover with black hair, and it fell around his eyes in tight curls. Nell signaled to my mother.

"His name is Lou Lubbock," she said. "For two dollars, he'll move the piano on his pickup truck."

By the time Mother had counted her change, Lou had rolled the piano up on a ramp into the back of the red pickup and was sitting in the cab beside a man whose face we couldn't see.

"Did you tell him where we live?" asked my mother.

"I told him to follow us," said Nell.

"You did?" exclaimed Mother. "Who's that old gentleman with him?"

"His father."

The piano, which had looked almost diminutive among the wardrobes and breakfronts at the auction, appeared monstrous when Lou tried to bring it through the front door of the cottage. Mother cast anxious glances at Lou Lubbock's father. He did not look as though he'd ever moved anything heavier than a telephone book.

"Won't go through the front door," he remarked, as the two men set the piano on the grass.

"I guess we'll have to take it back to the auction," said Mother. She sounded relieved.

"What doesn't go through the door goes through the window," said Lou. "Trust me."

With the practiced hand of a burglar, he pried out the top half of the big window in the living room and pushed his father through. Then he lifted the front end of the piano, letting it straddle the sill.

There was a sudden thud, and all at once the piano was standing in the living room as if it had always been there. As Lou Lubbock took his leave, somewhere between our front door and his truck, he invited Nell to go roller-skating.

That summer Nell kept company with the piano mover and I read *Tales of French Love and Passion* and mooned around the visible borders of their passion like a twelve-year-old voyeur. But when school started in September and our teacher asked us to write about what we did on our vacation, did I write about Aunt Nell and the piano mover? No. I wrote about the lake, the fish, and the turtles. What I learned about love that summer sank out of sight but not out of mind. Like so many visitors from the invisible world, those memories come unannounced and never when I call them.

Writers believe they choose the stories they want to write, but this is an illusion. Our stories choose us, and they are as patient and sure as the heroine in that tale I found on my aunt's nightstand. Not until ninth grade did I meet it again when I happened to check out of the school library a modest gray hardcover called *The Complete Stories of Guy de Maupassant*. As I reread it with astonishment and awe, the longing that had infused the summer of the piano mover washed over me. I wanted to write a love story. And Maupassant made it look so easy.

There are two ways of beginning such a story. The first lets you know right away that you're reading a love story. The second does not; indeed, it takes pains to hide its true intent. A beginning of the first kind can make you feel you're eavesdropping on a telephone with a party line. Here is the opening of John Updike's "Love Song for a Moog Synthesizer":

She was good in bed. She went to church. Her I.Q. was 145. She repeated herself. Nothing fit; it frightened him. Yet Tod wanted to hang on to the bits and pieces, which perhaps were not truly pieces but islands, which a little lowering sea level would reveal to be rises on a sunken continent, peaks of a sub-aqueous range, secretly one, a world.[2]

What Updike gives us is a close-up: the raw surface of the lover's confusion as he picks over the bits and pieces of a relationship, puzzling over them, gathering them into the lap of a long sentence, trying to understand love through the sum of its parts.

Now turn the telescope of the lover's vision around. The moment you step back and put a little distance between you and the characters, you have space to examine their motives, as Alice Walker does in the opening sentence of her story "The Lover": "Her husband had wanted a child and so she gave him one as a gift, because she liked her husband and admired him greatly."[3]

No writer can surpass Isaac Babel for opening sentences that perfectly balance distance with immediacy. Take the beginning a story called "First Love," which, by its very title, announces its subject—a dangerous practice for a novice writer:

When I was ten years old, I fell in love with a woman called Galina. Her surname was Rubtsov. Her husband, an officer, went off to the Russo-Japanese War and returned in October, 1905. He brought a great many trunks back with him. These trunks, which weighed nearly half a ton, contained Chinese souvenirs such as screens and costly weapons. Kuzma the yardman used to tell us that Rubtsov had bought all these things with money he had embezzled while serving in the engineer corps of the Manchurian Army.[4]

Though Babel's impassioned opening sentence seems to give the whole story away, he follows it, not with a description of Galina, but with three purely factual statements: her name, her husband's occupation, and what he brought home from the war. The last sentence in the paragraph turns from fact to rumor and gives us a little of the husband's character through the eyes of the yardman. The husband is a crook. Babel knows that part of telling a story well is holding back and that Chekhov's advice on writing about grief also applies to writing about love:

> When you . . . wish to move your reader to pity, try to be colder. It will give a kind of backdrop to . . . grief, make it stand out more. . . . Yes, be cold.[5]

Why am I seeking advice from Chekhov? Because Nell's story is knocking at a locked door in the back of my mind, and I can't find the key to let it out. The key is the right voice to tell it. Should the teller be a twelve-year-old child, narrating the events with an innocent eye? Or the child, grown up now, looking back? Should I tell it in the voice of my mother, looking askance? Or should I hand the story over to Aunt Nell, who is not looking at all but stepping headlong into love?

Here's one possible way into the story:

> The piano went for twenty-five dollars, plus three dollars extra if you wanted the auctioneer's assistant to move it. Nell asked him if would move it for two, as she and her sister were short of cash. Watching him push it up the ramp into his pickup truck, she thought, I could run away with that man.

The instant I've written these lines, I know I'm lying. It was not love at first sight. Every evening Lou Lubbock called for Nell in his pickup truck, and every night I dozed but did not fall asleep until two in the morning, when his truck clattered down the dirt road to our house, and Nell let herself in through the kitchen door, and my mother tiptoed downstairs in her nightgown. Together my mother and Nell sat in front of the empty fireplace and went over the day, piece by piece. A knothole in the floor under my bed gave me a clear view of the living room. If I pressed my ear to the hole, I could catch most of their conversation. It might go something like this:

> Mother: So where did he take you?
> Nell: We went roller-skating.

Mother: Oh, you love roller-skating.

Nell: Not with him. He's a terrible skater. All he wants to do is eat.

Mother: Where'd you eat?

Nell: He took me to the Harvest Table.

Mother: That's a nice restaurant.

Nell: But he chews with his mouth full. And he always has dirt under his nails. I said to him, "Lou, just because you work on cars all day doesn't mean you can't wash up afterwards."

Mother: Why do you go out with him?

Nell: Because he's there.

Oh, he was certainly there. Though he was always on her mind, she made it clear to us that she would leave him at the end of the summer. Even she would not have called whatever passed between them love.

Who knows better than Chekhov the power of love that begins with mild curiosity and ends with obsession? In "The Lady with the Pet Dog," a man has an affair with a woman he meets at a resort hotel, expecting to forget her when the affair ends, as he has forgotten other women. In a single paragraph, Chekhov shows us the lover's inability to forget:

A month or so would pass, and the image of Anna Sergeyevna, it seemed to him, would become misty in his memory, and only from time to time he would dream of her with her touching smile as he dreamed of others. But more than a month went by, winter came into its own, and everything was still clear in his memory as though he had departed from Anna Sergeyevna only yesterday. And his memories glowed more and vividly. . . . In the street he followed the women with his eyes, looking for someone who resembled her.[6]

After the summer ended, Nell rarely mentioned Lou Lubbock. A week before Christmas, one of the women who lived in the cottage next door called to say Lou's truck had skidded on a patch of ice and flipped over on him. "He was trapped for six hours before he died," she added. "Thank God he was alone when it happened."

That winter when Nell came to visit on weekends, I could feel the ghost of Lou Lubbock listening, invisible and helpless, as she told the story of how she'd met her first husband in the laundromat. She'd just put two quarters into the dyer.

> I went to get a Coke from the machine, and he snuck over and opened the door of the dryer and threw all his stuff in with mine. When we tried to sort it out, my bra was hooked around his undershirt. One thing sort of led to another.

Now let me interrupt myself with a story that I hope will illuminate the problem facing any writer who has ever set out to write a love story. Three years after the summer of Nell and the piano mover, my sister, who was living in a sorority house in Ann Arbor, accepted the fraternity pin of the boy she was dating, and called home, four blocks away, to announce the good news.

"I've been 'pinned'!"

I was fifteen and thought the choice of words was unfortunate; it made me think of wrestlers on a mat, of butterflies skewered under labels. But to those wiser than I, it meant she was one step away from being engaged. It also meant that on a Monday night in the middle of May the whole fraternity would assemble under her window and serenade her. Of course my mother and father and I were not invited. But she explained that if we brought binoculars and hid behind the trees or in the bushes that flourished in the front yard of the First Presbyterian Church across the street, we could get a good view of the whole ceremony.

On the appointed evening, my mother and father concealed themselves behind two large oaks, and I tucked myself into a honeysuckle bush between the church and the parking lot, with its single car, and waited for the show to begin. The fragrance of honeysuckle filled me with a nameless sorrow. Because I had the best view, my mother had entrusted me with the binoculars. The sorority house was dark save for a single upstairs window, at which my sister stood, holding a candle so that love could find her. Presently I heard the clatter of footsteps in the distance. What appeared to be a well-trained army of salesmen was marching toward my sister's light, two by two, on the opposite side of the street. They assembled under her window, and after a small silence—during which I could almost hear the squeak of a pitch-pipe—they burst into song.

A love song, no doubt. I've forgotten the words. In the middle of it, the young man paying court to my sister, held up something large and lobed—his heart, I thought, till it lit up and through the binoculars I saw it was a model of his fraternity pin. Was it my fear of the dark that made me turn the binoculars away from my sister to the parking lot? What did it matter if I had the worst view of the pinning ceremony? I had an extraordinary view of the couple necking in the car in the parking lot.

Writing a love story is a little like finding yourself with a pair of binoculars in your hand, caught between passion and scruples, ceremony and sex. If you err too far in either direction, you can end up on the side of pornography or romance. The difference between a love story and a romance is one of intent. When you write a romance, you carefully follow where many have trod, so that your readers can recognize the genre through its conventions. But in a love story, you try to show love as if your characters had just invented it. Follow your characters, and they will give you the story, but you can't tell ahead of time exactly where they'll lead you. Rousseau's advice for writing a love letter is also useful for writing a story: "You ought to begin without knowing what you mean to say, and to finish without knowing what you have written."

Love has its roots in the particular and the ordinary. Surely one of the writer's greatest challenges is to show how imagination can transform an ordinary human being into one whose absence turns day into night, heaven into hell, happiness into an abyss. Weather, light, fragrance, memory, and loneliness have more to do with the alchemy of love than beauty or grace; Maurice Chevalier once remarked that many a man has fallen in love with a girl in a light so dim he would not have chosen a suit by it. For showing that alchemy, I know of few writers who can surpass Thomas Mann in this passage from "Tonio Kröger":

> Strange how things come about! He had seen her a thousand times; then one evening he saw her again; saw her in a certain light, talking with a friend in a certain saucy way, laughing and tossing her head; saw her lift her arm and smooth her back hair with her schoolgirl hand, that was by no means particularly fine or slender, in such a way that the thin white sleeve slipped down from her elbow; heard her speak a word or two, a quite indifferent phrase, but with a certain intonation, with a warm ring in her voice, and his heart throbbed with ecstasy.[7]

We are in love, and love what vanishes; isn't that why the sight a thin white sleeve slipping down a girl's arm can break someone's heart? While lovers lie in each other's arms, the world is singing an older tune: "Golden lads and girls all must / As chimney-sweepers, come to dust."

But though the teller vanishes, the tale does not. Several years ago when I started to work on a novel called *Sister Water,* the voices of women—in the living room at two in the morning, these voices I thought I'd forgotten—did not forget me. As I wrote the chapter in which the main character receives word that her husband has been killed in a car accident, I knew what Aunt Nell would say.

"Death is so ordinary," she whispers. "Write about love."

NOTES

1. *Stories of Love and Passion: A Collection of Complete Short Stories Chosen from the Works of Guy de Maupassant.* No publication information is given in this edition. "Room Eleven" is included in *Miss Harriett and Other Stories,* Ernest August Boyd, trans. (New York: Knopf, 1923).

2. John Updike, "Love Song, for a Moog Synthesizer," *Problems and Other Stories* (New York: Knopf, 1979), p. 174.

3. Alice Walker, "The Lover," *You Can't Keep a Good Woman Down* (New York: Harcourt Brace Jovanovich), p. 237.

4. Isaac Babel, "First Love," *The Collected Stories of Isaac Babel* (New York: Criterion, 1955), p. 265.

5. Henri Troyat, *Chekhov,* Michael Henry Heim, trans. (New York: Dutton, 1986), p. 148.

6. *The Portable Chekhov,* Avrahm Yarmolinsky, ed. (New York: Viking, 1975), pp. 423–24.

7. Thomas Mann, "Tonio Kröger," *Death in Venice and Seven Other Stories,* translated from the German by H. T. Lowe-Porter (New York: Vintage, 1955), p. 85.

Put It on the Back Burner

SOME YEARS AGO I was teaching a class in writing poetry during which somebody raised the question of a poet's relationship to his or her muse. We had been reading a poem by Donald Justice, in which he describes his muse as a worldly seductress and a far cry from the angelic guardian Milton invokes at the beginning of *Paradise Lost.* After we talked about the muse as a power who watches over writers and inspires them, I gave the students an assignment. The assignment was: Describe your muse.

Lest anyone find this old-fashioned, I gave lip service to the famous nine, those daughters of Mnemosyne who inspired the ancient Greeks, and then I told my students to forget the daughters, but not their mother, whose common name is Memory. We are not talking about classical Muses here, I said. We are talking about your muse. Your *doppelgänger.* Your familiar. We are talking about the source of your inspiration, your vision.

The variety of muses the students came up with would have done credit to Hieronymus Bosch. They included animals both tame and wild, favorite pens and notebooks, men and women with wings and without them. When I gave myself the assignment, for I often do the assignments along with my students, I hardly dared tell them the truth. My muse is a stove.

Let me say right now that I am not one of those women who has spent much of her life slaving over a hot stove. In fact, I never learned to cook until I got married. After a month of hot dogs every night, my new husband asked if I had a cookbook. Hadn't somebody given us *The Joy of Cooking* for a wedding present? Somebody had, and it was full of useful information for the advanced cook.

But cooking was no joy to me when it involved directions—for, let us say, a sunshine cake—so detailed they might have been intended for an alchemist, trying to change lead into gold. Following the recipe in our local newspaper for easy chewy macaroons was about as simple as planning a wedding, in which a single misstep can lead to disaster. After my chewy macaroons had the unexpected effect of dislodging a guest's dentures, I vowed to find a cookbook that started with the basics: Face the stove.

So I bought a cookbook for children. An editor had told me that when grown-ups want the clearest possible instructions for anything from carpentry to cooking, they go straight to the children's room of the local public library. From the children's cookbook, I chose a familiar dish, the basic meatloaf. Unlike the *Joy of Cooking,* the children's cookbook had lot of pictures, and the writer had very sensibly broken the procedure into steps. Cooking was as easy as learning the samba. Step 1, step 2, step 3. I stepped out on the dance floor of the kitchen and was getting along pretty well until I hit the instructions for baking the meatloaf. They were as clear as a traffic light. They read: HAVE YOUR MOTHER HELP YOU LIGHT THE STOVE.

To a child, that means, "Get help until you get more experience." To an adult, whose mother has been dead for twenty years, it means, "Just do it." Lighting the stove is not so different from facing the blank page and starting a new poem, a new story.

By this time you have figured out for yourselves that the stove I call my muse is not a microwave or any of those gleaming electric ranges with timers that chime to let you know, with mathematical precision, when the sunshine cake or the meatloaf is done. No, my muse is a woodstove with four burners and an oven. In the morning you light it and in the evening you bank the embers, an act so important that the Irish have a ritual called "smooring the fire," which lets you enlist the aid of spiritual forces. Ask for the blessing at night and the fire will never go out.

Now, the burners on most stoves look as much alike as the keys on a piano. But watching my mother cook, I discovered there were subtle differences. On the front burners she cooked what needed immediate attention, that is, the vegetables we would be eating for supper that night. She lifted the lids, tasted the contents, and adjusted the heat high or low, according to what she found there. The back burner, which she turned low, was left to its own devices. The wonderful odor of things simmering and being allowed to perfect themselves in their own inexact time, came from the covered pot on the back burner.

Only once on the back burner of my grandmother's stove did I ever see the secret contents exposed. Two chicken legs, still armored with toenails, protruded from her pot of soup-in-progress, though she had clapped the lid on them. I always supposed that the pot on the back burner was covered to hide the raw and unpromising ingredients before their transformation into a stew or a soup or a pot roast so languid that the meat fell from the bone in thin strips and the marrow turned to a clear, rich jelly.

Cooking is magic, of course. You assemble the raw ingredients, you follow the directions, and if you are a good cook, you make exactly what you set out to make. This is the achievement of the front burner. It's only the inept or absent-minded cook who has to deal with unpleasant surprises.

The back burner, in my experience, is quite another matter. If Heraclitus could have dined at our house, I doubt he could have dipped his spoon into the same soup twice. There is not a writer alive who has not said to herself or himself, when a story or poem is going badly, "I'll put it on the back burner," that place of astonishing changes, and waited for the piece to become what it was destined to be, out of your sight and in the fullness of unmeasured time. The doctrine of the back burner is, "Out of sight is not out of mind." You don't forget about the poem or the story. You just let it forget about you.

So for better or worse, my muse is neither goddess nor angel but a wood stove.

Now I hear somebody asking, "Why not an electric stove?" If

an electric stove appears to you in a dream and offers to serve as your muse, say yes, and you can be sure it will come trailing clouds of memories, without which the back burner can do no work at all. The stove I call my muse has assembled itself from many memories.

Part of it belongs to the stove in the kitchen of the elderly woman who taught me how to sew. She lived on a farm outside of Owosso, Michigan, and she was so frugal that she mended the gaps in her uninsulated farmhouse with old paper Domino sugar sacks cut open and tacked neatly to the walls, like wallpaper done in palimpsest. She fed her stove wood when she could get it and old corncobs when she could not.

And so I learned that there are many ways of lighting a stove and many ways of keeping the flame alive. Keeping the flame alive—that's the most important thing, for both the writer and the cook. And because the writer who is on fire with an idea also wishes that the words would flow like water, my muse is never far from a well—and not one of those cheap wishing wells that one sees in suburban yards containing a pot of petunias and no water, like a relic from the time when people believed that a copper coin thrown into the well could persuade the spirit who lived there to do your bidding.

No, I want a real well, full of darkness and danger. Think of the fairy tales, in which a fall down a well or a rabbit hole leads not to death but another kind of life. The transformations that take place could not happen without this time spent out of sight of the ordinary world. Time out of sight of the world—that's what the back-burner gives our work. How can the poem or story evolve until it risks leaving the beaten path and setting out on an unexpected journey? Think of the heroine who loses her way in the forest, and only then does her life turn into a story worth telling.

The secret of the back burner is the power to transform a disaster into a miracle, whether it be to pare an unwieldly poem down to its best lines or to find the right voice for telling a tale that has haunted you for years.

But now I hear somebody ask, How does the back burner do

its work? The best way I can answer that question is to take an example from my own work, for which I apologize; there are far better collections of poems for children than the one I'll talk about, but I don't know the history of the creative process behind those collections. So I must turn to a book of poems for children whose history I do know. The book describes life at a celestial diner and cafe, and it is called *The Moon & Riddles Diner and the Sunnyside Café*.

Long before I wrote the book, I had developed a passion for odd names. Names in telephone books of people I've never met, names in the zip code directory of places I've never visited, foreign names that roll off my tongue and away from their meanings. To me, these names suggest characters who might have stories to tell.

I put my idea for the book on the back burner and by way of stirring the pot now and then, I thought about who these characters were. I wanted some plucky heroine, someone the reader could identify with, but I had no idea where I would find her. Until I could hear her voice in my head, it would be impossible to write her story.

So I also put my wish for a plucky heroine on the back burner and forgot about her—until the hot afternoon in July there came a loud knock at the front door. When I opened it I was facing a Girl Scout with black-rimmed glasses and stringy blond hair who did not care if her uniform was neat and who wasn't wearing a sash covered with badges. When she gave me the sales pitch for Oreos and oatmeal cookies, I remarked, "There are a lot more kinds available than when I sold Girl Scout cookies." She said nothing, but her glance said, "You can't fool me. You never sold Girl Scout cookies." She knew her own mind and there was no changing it. Business was business.

When I ordered two boxes of oatmeal cookies, she took off her backpack and pulled out her notepad and wrote up the order. She did not say thank you. And I couldn't get her out of my head.

Two weeks later she delivered the cookies and wormed her way into *The Moon & Riddles Diner*. How did a cocky Girl Scout cookies salesgirl find her way into my book? And where had I met her before? If not the same girl, maybe one of her ancestors? Where did my plucky heroine's voice come from? I found the answer when my eye fell on a stanza from a favorite Mother Goose song I'd taped to the door of our refrigerator so many years ago that I'd forgotten it was there.

> I went to the river—
> No ship to get across,
> I paid ten shillings
> For an old blind horse;
> I up on his back
> And off in a crack,
> Sally tell my mother
> I shall never come back.

The back burner makes connections between great and small, far and near, silly and solemn. You take what it gives you, and you use it. You remember that when I told my students about the Greek Muses, I said, "Forget about the famous nine but don't forget their mother." Their mother, you will recall, is Memory, without which no muse can function. That stanza was a door, but it was Memory who opened the door to the place where the dish runs away with the spoon. A message deeply encoded into the nonsense of Mother Goose is one that young children understand because it touches their own experience of the world, a world in which everything is alive.

But now I hear somebody ask, "Does the back burner do nothing but turn over early memories? Can it transform the conversation you overheard yesterday or the article you read in the newspaper this morning?" And my answer is, that is exactly what the back burner does best. Its motto is *Carpe Diem*. If you want to use the past, look to the present. The catalyst that focuses the amorphous brew of memories into a poem or a story can be as huge as a cyclone or as fleeting as a conversation with a Girl Scout.

Every writer has fantasized about the perfect reader, the person you would most like to see reading your book. You will never guess mine, so I'd better tell you. The setting is a diner in a small town, somewhere in the Midwest. It's midnight, the diner has closed, and the customers have all gone home. The waitress has left her copy of *The Moon & Riddles Diner and the Sunnyside Café* on the counter. She'll remember it later and pick it up in the morning.

But now, at midnight, a dish and a spoon are huddled over the book. The dish is reading it to the spoon. Suddenly the stove, who they thought was asleep, calls out, "Hey, that part about the back burner—could you read that part again?"

Camping on the Border

I'VE BEEN ASKED to speak about my life as a writer, but my life thus far would hardly make a story worth reading, and I've always taken that old adage, Write from what you know, to mean something else. Write from more than you know.

So let's talk instead about the writer's life, which we are all involved in, and where we can meet on common ground.

Several years ago I was flying to Fairbanks, Alaska, for a writers' conference on a plane that made a stop in Salt Lake City. A dozen fresh-faced young men got on, dressed in black suits. At first glance I took them to be a group of undertakers, bound, perhaps for a conference also, but at second glance I realized they looked too cheerful and too young to have death on their minds. Perhaps they were tourists, I thought, outward bound for new territories, new experiences.

But does one set out for new experiences and new territories in a black wool suit? No doubt they're salesmen, I decided. And when one of the young men took the seat next to me, I realized that I wasn't far off when he explained that he was a Mormon going out on his mission, to spread the word of God.

Then he turned to me and asked, "And what do you do?"

There seemed no single answer to this. Should I answer by telling him that I am a college teacher and that I have taught writing, medieval literature, and a class in the history of fairy tales for grown-ups? Or should I say, I'm a wife and mother who writes fiction and poetry? Or should I say, I am a writer, spreading the word, but not, I think, the word of God, though once in a while He will show up in one of my poems or stories and comment on human affairs, though never with a view to making the human race behave itself. Since I was on my way to a writers' conference, I said,

"I'm a writer."

The young man looked at me with as much curiosity as if I had been a platypus.

"And is this what writers do?" he asked. "Travel around?"

I was about to say, "Do you think books write themselves? Writers sit in front of computers or typewriters or stacks of paper, and they write."

What stopped me was the thought that in some way he had hit on the truth. Writers do travel around, though much of the travel takes place in their heads as they are standing in line at the supermarket, or walking to and from the library. Writers who interrupt work on a poem to get dinner on the table have fits of absent-mindedness. Like the time my head was so full of a poem in progress that I left my hairbrush in the refrigerator, thus causing my husband and son to fear that my cooking had reached an all-time low. Sherwood Anderson said that writers do much of their work in bed, working the story out in their minds before committing it to paper.

There are two kinds of journeys we all make. The first is the journey that you can map. Your destination is clear, the map will show you the shortest way to get from here to there. The second kind is the journey where you go by instinct. Not even a compass will help you. In my family we had travelers who tried both kinds. Before we set out on any long family trip, my father would stop by AAA and pick up the maps, on which his route was carefully marked in red. Dad always kept a map in his car. My aunt kept a map in her car, too, but if she started daydreaming and got lost, which happened quite often, she'd pitch the map into the back seat and say, "This map has gone bad on us." She'd take the long way home, the scenic route, you might say.

The journeys that writers make are like both kinds. Sometimes you need the map. When you are revising your work, it's helpful to know where you're going and how you plan to get there. But when you're writing a first draft—ah, that's a different story.

The truth is, writers live on the interface of two worlds, the world that gives us dreams, poems, and stories, and the world that gives us jobs, book contracts, and money. Sometimes we live on the tension between them the way water striders scoot on the surface of water that is both a roof to the fish and a floor to the water bugs. Writers are like referees trying to keep two players on track so that the game can move forward, even though each player is playing with different rules. The game is called Making Time, and it's World versus Dream. World understands the measure of minutes and hours. World sets up deadlines and carries maps. World signs contracts. Dream is allergic to time and has long ago given up wearing a watch. Dream is a hunter who can wait years for a glimpse of what she lives for. Even when she doesn't know what she wants, she knows she will recognize it when she meets it. She carries no map and the only compass she follows is her own heart.

How many of us have said, "If I only had a block of time, I could finish this book." How many writers, suddenly given the gift of time, find that the story or poem has other plans and that the vision eludes them? I believe it is not talent but the experience of failure and the capacity to learn from failure and to make something out of it that determines who will survive the journey to becoming a writer, and that journey is different for everyone. It's a lesson you have to learn over and over. Most of the writers I know will tell you that for every published book, there are five unpublished ones in the back room that helped clear a path for the one that finally worked. For writers, getting stuck means learning to write as much of the story as you know, then letting go of it, knowing that letting go is not giving up. It is listening for the still small voice of the story, laying aside your own plans for it, and watching it choose its own direction, very much like a dream that seems to make no sense, yet does in fact make uncommon sense. You are not writing from what you know. You are writing from more than you know.

Let's assume that all the pieces of the book you want to write have come together You are ready to write it. But what if the book you want to write is not one for which someone will pay you a year's wages? You know that a block of uninterrupted time is what you really need. I know a few brave souls who took the plunge and set out to support themselves with their writing, and they deserve our everlasting admiration. Earlier I told you that I am a teacher, and of course teaching takes time from my writing. But it also connects me to a community of lively young minds who I'm sure have taught me as much about human nature and its possibilities as I've taught them. The very act of teaching can be humbling. Whether you are a cook or a poet or a pilot, you have no idea how imperfect your knowledge of your craft is until you try teaching it to somebody else. You also learn a lot about the value of time and how not to waste it.

But more important, for me the teaching job that encroaches on my writing time also protects the part of me from which poems and stories come. It allows me to focus on the writing, not on the marketplace. It allows me to take risks and fail, to take on projects that pay little but push me beyond my comfortable habits of writing into new material and new way of working. A couple of years ago, an editor at Simon and Schuster contacted me about a wonderful idea she had for a book. And what was this wonderful idea? A retelling of *Paradise Lost* for children, she said.

Paradise Lost? I said. Surely I'd misheard her.

Oh, yes, she said. It's a great story. Children will love it.

I was on the verge of saying, "Have you lost your wits?" when the still small voice of Dream said, "Go ahead, try it. You know that poem well. You've taught it to Vassar freshman. Here's your chance to save Eve's reputation. You remember all that stuff Milton wrote about the inferiority of women. Here's your chance to set the story straight."

So I agreed to write it, but only if I didn't have to write it in poetry and if I could include as much of Milton's imagery and language as possible. But I didn't want my version of *Paradise Lost* to read like a rewrite of Cliffs Notes. Rereading Milton's poem, sifting each line for what I would save and what I would leave behind, was much harder than simply translating it into another language. I couldn't add scenes that Milton hadn't written—that would be cheating—but in my telling I could reinterpret him. Retelling *Paradise Lost* was like taking a trip to some rarely visited part of the world. You leave all the comforts of home behind. It takes a long time to get there and the roads are nonexistent so you have to make most of the journey on foot. Afterwards you are glad you made the trip but you would not want to do it again.

And how did I manage to save Eve's reputation and still stay true to Milton? In Books 11 and 12, the archangel Michael arrives and explains to Adam the consequences of the Fall by narrating the future history of the world: Cain kills Abel, the flood kills nearly everybody, the Exodus from Egypt follows, along with Abraham, Moses, the prophets, the Crucifixion, the redemption of humanity, the end of time, and the arrival of a new heaven and a new earth.

Eve hears none of this. Not wishing to burden the intellect of the weaker sex, Michael puts her to sleep. It is understood that Adam will give her a summary of the main points. The archangel then proceeds to talk for forty-seven pages (in my edition). When Michael departs and Eve wakes up, she tells Adam there's no need to tell her the whole story. She already knows it. She speaks for the artists and writers who will live after her and who will understand that reason is not the only road to truth. Eve has gone down that road not taken, the shortcut, the scenic route, the Road of Intuition.

> Whence thou return'st and whither went'st, I know;
> For God is also in sleep, and Dreams advise[1]

Milton would be less amazed at my conclusion here than at the process of publishing my version of *Paradise Lost*.

The editor's choice of an illustrator for the book demonstrates how faxes and e-mails and computers have changed the face of publishing—and for the better. The illustrator lives in South

Africa and has no plans to visit the United States. I have no plans to visit South Africa. We will probably never meet, except in Paradise and Hell on the pages of this book, God willing. And maybe God is willing. After all, he's in it.

I once heard a very fine and very successful illustrator talk about choices and decisions he'd had the opportunity to make that would help further his "career." That any artist, whether a writer or an illustrator, could even speak of his art as a career filled me with awe. Most of the events in my life that have helped me as a writer have come by accident, from good luck and from editors willing to taking risks on projects that looked far from promising and came within a hair's breadth of never getting into print at all. One such project was a manuscript called *A Visit to William Blake's Inn,* which I would never have written if Barbara Lucas, an editor at Harcourt with whom I'd worked on many other books had not said to me, "How about writing a collection of poems for children?"

I had never written a collection of poems for children and hardly knew how to go about it. My books of poetry for adults were written in the way such books are usually written. For several years you publish poems in this quarterly, in that review, in this little magazine, with a lot of rejections on the way, and at some point you make a selection and arrange them, and send the manuscript out into the world. Nobody comes knocking at your door, asking for a book of poems.

But for children's books, it's a different story. The poems in a collection for children are often related, either by subject or theme, and for this reason the poems might be written all at one go, not over the long period that the adult collection requires. Seeing my bewilderment, Barbara made some suggestions to get me started.

"How about a book of poems about the seasons?"

I said I'd think about it. And I did think about it, for about one minute. But my best work comes, not when I choose the idea, but when the idea chooses me. Sometimes you're lucky, and the editor's request triggers your imagination and sends you forth on a journey you would not have taken if you hadn't been asked. So when Barbara asked me to write a collection of poems for children, I left the door open and waited to see what would fly through.

And now I have to stop and tell you a little about how I work. Ever since I was a small child, I have always made things with my hands, to help me take my eye off the story so it can find out what it wants to be. If the story I'm working on is a fairy tale, I will often make the characters to help me understand who they are. It's not that different from the way I use to pretend inanimate things were alive when I was a child, arranging great dramas on the dining room table with a large cast of salt cellars, spoons, and spice bottles. Sometimes the character my hands have made gives me the idea for a poem or a story. The characters are always made out of found material, scraps of cloth, feathers, crab claws, erasers, old kitchen implements, soda cans, and while I work I listen to music or poetry on tape.

It so happened that when Barbara asked me to write a book of poems for children I was building a house out of cardboard boxes, a house only six feet tall and far more orderly than the house I live in. While I made the house and its inhabitants I was listening to Blake's poetry being read on tape. The poems were inspired by both of these activities. Since many writers find that working with your hands has a good effect on working with your head, I no longer apologize for playing with sticks and stones and messing around with odd materials. Furthermore, I can blame it on neoteny—a very useful word, which puts these activities in a flattering light. I discovered this word in a book called *Teaching Photography,* by Philip Perkis. Here's his description of how he discovered the meaning of neoteny:

> When I was leaving my full-time teaching job last fall, I was speaking with John Levine on the telephone. John is a psychiatrist, who teaches at Harvard Medical School. He was in the first photography class I taught and became interested in the

relationship between photographic, musical and emotional tone.

I told John I had a strange feeling, although 65 and retiring, part of me still doesn't know "what I want to be when I grow up." "That's neoteny," John said. He went on to explain that neoteny is a biological term which is used metaphorically to describe adults who, while functioning at a mature level, retain and utilize traits from earlier stages of development: curiosity; imagination; playfulness; a zest for learning new things; and a connection with childhood feelings and fantasies. Many older artists are in that situation, he said. "It's a positive adaptation. It's also part of how they got to be artists in the first place."[2]

I am sure Barbara was surprised to find William Blake instead of the seasons, but she graciously accepted the poems and sent the manuscript to Alice and Martin Provensen to illustrate. At no time was I or Barbara allowed to see the work in progress. As Martin said to me, "If you showed in your face you didn't like what we are doing, it would be very hard to go back to the drawing board." But I'd loved their work for years and the illustrations for this book exceeded my wildest expectations. The Provensens had looked at portraits of Blake, and the poet they paint is indeed William himself, red haired and bright-eyed.

Do I make the process of putting this book into the world sound easy? It wasn't. The road to publication was a bumpy one, as it is for many books. The head of the trade division was replaced by a young woman with limited experience in the publishing business who took one look at *A Visit to William Blake's Inn,* marched into Barbara's office, and demanded to know why this book was being published. Who would buy it? Who among potential buyers would have even heard of William Blake? Better to cancel the contract and kill the book than to bring out something with no commercial future at all.

Barbara reminded the young woman that a contract is a contract, and Harcourt had agreed to publish the book. Not long after this, my editor got fired and was replaced by the copy editor, who had very little knowledge of either poetry or Blake and no affection for this book.

It was only after the book had won the Newbery that Martin Provensen told me what he assumed was the reason the publisher did not cancel it. The artwork had been handed in two weeks before. The book was ready to go to press. Had this not been so, who knows if that book would ever have been published?

The call from the chairperson of the Newbery committee, which came in the middle of dinner, was so unexpected that she had to call twice. The connection was bad, the voice broken up, the message garbled, and when my nine-year-old son answered the phone, he could make nothing of it, and he hung up.

"Who was it?" I asked.

"It sounded like Big Bird," he said, and we all went back to eating dinner. The second time the phone rang, I answered it, all ready to utter some rude remark to the person making a crank call.

This time, the message came through.

One of the unexpected effects of winning the Newbery was that I was now labeled as a writer of children's books. I have never thought of myself as a children's book writer, but simply as a writer, since the first books I wrote were for adults and I have never stopped writing for that audience. But I have always read illustrated books for children, because it seems a great pity that so few adult books of fiction and poetry contain pictures. For centuries texts and images belonged together. William Blake was so convinced of this that when he was preparing the pages for *Songs of Innocence* and *Songs of Experience,* he engraved each poem and picture on a single plate, so they would not be separated.

INTRODUCTION

Piping down the valleys wild
Piping songs of pleasant glee,
On a cloud I saw a child
And he laughing said to me:

"Pipe a song about a Lamb!"
So I piped with merry chear.

"Piper, pipe that song again;"
So I piped, he wept to hear.

"Drop thy pipe, thy happy pipe;
Sing thy songs of happy chear."
So I sung the same again
While he wept with joy to hear.

"Piper, sit thee down and write
"In a book that all may read."
So he vanish'd from my sight
And I pluck'd a hollow reed

And I made a rural pen,
And I stain'd the water clear,
And I wrote my happy songs
Every child may joy to hear.[3]

Was Blake writing for children or grown-ups? Would he have written the poems differently if a publisher had said to him, "Now, Mr. Blake, give us a book of poems for children"? Of course not. One of my touchstones as a writer is W. H. Auden's observation on the difference between children's books and adult books: "There are good books which are only for adults because their comprehension presupposes adult experience, but there are no good books which are only for children."[4] And the writer about whom Auden made this remark? It was Lewis Carroll.

In the world of publishing, marketing people are keenly aware that adults do read children's books, but alas, they also find that when a manuscript suitable for both adults and children is published as a book for children, it rarely finds its way to adult readers. The Harry Potter books crossed that boundary, and thank heaven for that. Our local paper ran a notice that the British edition of the fifth Harry Potter book was published with two different covers, one for adults and one for children. The children's edition shows a bright red and orange phoenix rising from the flames. The adult version features a more subdued cover, showing a somber black and white phoenix, so that adults can read it in public and not be caught enjoying a children's book with nary a child in sight.

Having stated these bleak tidings, I would advise you to pay no attention to them. Write the stories you want to write. Think of yourself as the village storyteller, telling your tales and your poems to old and young, north and south, east and west. You are writing for readers who will pick up your book tomorrow and readers who will discover it a hundred years from tomorrow. Don't disappoint them.

NOTES

1. John Milton, *Paradise Lost,* Merritt Y. Hughes, ed. (New York: Odyssey Press, 1935), p. 410.

2. Philip Perkis, *Teaching Photography* (Rochester, New York: OB Press, 2001), p. 73.

3. William Blake, "Introduction," *Complete Writings,* Geoffrey Keynes, ed. (Oxford: Oxford University Press, 1972), p. 111.

4. W. H. Auden, "Lewis Carroll," *Forewords and Afterwords,* Edward Mendelson, ed. (New York: Random House, 1973), p. 291.

Players in the Minor League

⌒∞⌒

I.

ONCE UPON A TIME when I was five years old and it was twenty below zero in Ann Arbor, Michigan, and six feet of snow had closed the kindergarten and not even the cat was allowed outside, a delicate knock brushed our front door. My mother opened it and there stood a short elderly woman with a dark, exquisite face.

"Can I come in and warm myself?" she asked. She told us her name was Lily Lee Moore and this was her day to clean Mr. Knight's house two doors down from ours, but Mr. Knight had gone out and locked all his doors, and she did not have the key to any of them. Her connection with Mr. Knight made our visitor as exotic as if she'd dropped from a distant star. We did not have a cleaning woman and our only dealings with Mr. Knight took place one summer evening when our dog ran off with a flank steak he had imprudently left on his outdoor grill, intending to broil it for dinner. While my mother was washing the supper dishes, she caught sight of Mr. Knight's cook, in a white apron, wrestling the steak from the jaws of our playful collie. Mr. Knight himself did not honor us with a personal appearance.

My mother led Lily Lee Moore into the living room, offered her a chair by the fireplace, and went off to make a cup of tea for her, leaving me to entertain our guest. What interested me, I thought, could not fail to interest her. I had just set up my Noah's ark on the coffee table, and while the tea was brewing, I introduced her to Mr. and Mrs. Noah and their sudden influx of birds and beasts, grand-marching two by two into the ark. As I set up the characters, I told her the story as it had been read to me in Bible school. *And Noah went in, and his sons and his wife, and his son's wives with him, into the ark, because of the waters of the flood.* And the animals went in, two by two.

Lily Lee Moore listened politely. At the end of my story, she said, "You left a lot of stuff out."

I was dumbfounded.

"What did I leave out?"

"All those people who couldn't get into the ark—what do you think they did while the water was rising?

To this day the memory of her voice, with its burden of fear and loss, has stayed with me. *The river's rising and rising, and now the water's up to the windows of the stores downtown. There ain't nobody left in the Paradise Bar, they're all looking for high ground. Whole families are a-climbing the trees, just sitting up there in the forks of the maples, looking down and watching the water. They can see it carrying big branches with the green leaves still on 'em and cars and rooftops right along, right along, and the water is up to the first fork of those trees, and pretty soon they see it's carrying the bodies of drowned people, and now the water is up to the second fork of the trees, and a woman looks down and says, "Lordy, Lordy, here come the dead." The water is carrying coffins, some of 'em open and the corpses gone. And now it's dark and the wind is roaring and the water is nipping the last fork, and there ain't nothing in sight but the tops of the trees. The last woman on earth—I ain't counting Noah and his kin, 'cause they're on the water, not in it—the last woman on earth looks out and sees the dark sea, rocking and tossing, and she thinks, "They're gonna make it through, and I ain't."*

And then the water slurps over her and there ain't another living thing that'll make it through this storm except the folks in the ark.

Beyond the living room window, icicles bared their teeth. Lily Lee Moore, safe in the ark of our house, sipped her tea and warmed her feet in front of the fire. And I have Lily Lee Moore to thank for my first lesson in the art of fiction.

Or more specifically, my first lesson in point of view. It took me a long time to realize that she'd added nothing to the story that wasn't already there. Any traditional tale gives you three kinds of characters. The main characters are important enough to have names. The minor characters have names, of course, but often the storyteller chooses not to give them. In the story of the ark, Noah's sons are named, but all the women are clumped together under a single noun: the wives. The moment you name a minor character, he or she is minor no more.

When writers begin to fiddle with those traditional stories, the minor characters see their chance for glory. Though Noah is the hero, it's hard to identify with someone whom God has designated as the most righteous man on the planet. The righteous man may save us from our follies but he doesn't help us laugh at them. It's no accident that when the pageant of *Noah's Flood* was performed during the sixteenth century in England, Noah's wife upstaged her husband, not because she was virtuous but because she was human. She speaks for all of us when she shouts,

> I will not out of this town.
> But I have my gossips every one, [unless; friends]
> One foot further I will not gone; [go]
> And I may save their life. [if]
> They love me full well, by Christ;
> But thou wilt let them in thy chest, [ark]
> Else row forth, Noah, whither thou list, [wishes]
> And get thee a new wife.[1]

Four hundred years later, she has a name: Mrs. Noah. When Glen Rounds writes a book called *Washday on Noah's Ark,* he leaves God out and focuses on how Mrs. Noah copes with the problem of drying forty days and forty nights' worth of laundry on an ark without a clothesline. *Norah's Ark,* by Ann Cartwright, gets rid of both Noah and God. We have lost a Noah but gained a Norah. In a godless world, Norah is, nevertheless, the Mother Superior of the animals on her farm. She hears a flood warning on the radio and is struck by the obvious solution: build a boat. No mean carpenter, this Norah: she flips her barn over, stays up all night hammering new walls and making a roof. In the morning she tells the animals, "Let's call our boat Norah's Ark," and she sings, "The animals went in one by one." The ark is inconvenient but cozy. The story ends where it began. Nobody drowns. No promises, no rainbow.

Contemporary fiction for both adults and children includes so many offbeat retellings and "fractured fairy tales" that the tale of Norah's ark hardly raises an eyebrow. Main characters change their identities or their genders, ogres complain of ogre abuse at the hands of plucky princes, the big bad wolf turns out to be a vegetarian. I have read many of these tales, chuckled over some and forgotten others. But Lily Lee Moore's description of the last woman on earth I have not forgotten. She is neither a main character nor a minor character. The last woman on earth belongs to the third kind of character: the one whom the storyteller has not shown us, the witness we know is present, watching the main action. All these people who couldn't get into the ark—*what do you think they did while the water was rising?*

Many years after hearing Lily Lee Moore's story, I am haunted by the image of Mr. Knight sailing off in an ark he has had custom-built to his specifications. He does not invite us to join him. Is death by boredom preferable to death by water? Mr. Knight does not like dogs, and he would be dreadful company on so long a voyage; the only story he knows is his own. Any writer who takes Henry James' advice seriously, "Try to be one of the people on whom nothing is lost!"[2] will end up, sooner or later, looking for the hidden story, hidden because nobody was listening for it, and because the water is rising, and because there but for the grace of God go you and I.

II.

I like to imagine the sons and daughters of Noah passing the long days on the water by telling each other stories. *Their* stories, not Noah's. In fairy tales, it's the minor characters I love best. They are usually odder and noisier and funnier than those who play out their lives on the main stage, and best of all, their stories have not yet been told.

And why do I care about these characters who were not deemed worthy even to have names?

When I was in high school, I joined the Thespians Club, not because I had any great talent for acting but because I had just cracked up the driver's education car—our school had only one—and I wanted an excuse to quit the class before worse befell me. The Thespians met every week after school at exactly the same time as driver's ed, and I figured the theater was safer and less stressful. There would be something I could do, even if it was just passing out the programs.

I did not even have to audition for my first role in a play whose author and title I have forgotten. Somebody was needed to play the maid, who crosses the stage at the beginning of act 1, shakes her feather duster at invisible motes in the spotlight, exits into the wings, and is never seen again. When the school put on *The Pirates of Penzance,* I was the invisible alto in the back row of the chorus. When I played in the school orchestra, mine was the last chair in the violin section. What all this gave me was not a sense of failure, but an appreciation for the unspoken passions of the minor characters in fiction.

Let me introduce you to two of my favorites that appear in a fairy tale from the Brothers Grimm. It is called "The Raven." In the story a young man sets out to free a princess, who tells him that to do so he must come to the golden castle of Mount Stromberg. Here follows one of the strangest scenes you will find in any fairy tale.

So he stood up and set out for the golden castle of Mount Stromberg, even though he did not know where it was. After he had wandered about the world for a long time, he finally came to a dark forest and continued wandering for fourteen days. When he realized that he could not find his way out, he lay down exhausted on the fourteenth evening and fell asleep under a bush. The next day he moved on, and in the evening, as he was about to lie down under another bush, he heard such a moaning and groaning that he was unable to sleep. When the hour came for people to light their lamps, he saw a light glimmering in the distance, got up, and went toward it. Shortly after, he came to a house that appeared to be very small because a big giant was standing in front of it. If you try to go inside, he thought to himself, and the giant catches sight of you, he'll put an end to your life. Finally, he decided to risk it and stepped toward the door. When the giant saw him, he said, "It's good that you've come. I haven't had a thing to eat for a long time. So I'm going to gobble you up for supper."

"You'd better not," said the man. "I don't like to be gobbled up. If you want something to eat, I have enough here to fill your stomach."

"If that's true," said the giant, "you can rest easy. I wanted to eat you only because I had nothing else."

They went in and sat down at the dinner table, and the man took out the bread, wine, and meat that never ran out.

"I like this very much," said the giant, and he ate to his heart's content.

After supper the man asked him, "Can you tell me the location of the golden castle of Mount Stromberg?"

The giant said, "I'll look it up on my map. It shows all the cities, villages, and houses." He got out a map that he kept in the room and looked for the castle, but it was not on it. "Don't worry," he said. "I've got even larger maps in the closet upstairs. We can look for it on them." Yet, it was all in vain.

Now, the man wanted to move on, but the giant begged him to stay a few more days until his brother returned. He had merely gone out to fetch some provisions. When the brother came back, they asked him about the golden castle of Mount Stromberg.

"When I'm finished eating," he answered, "I'll look it up on the map."

A little later he climbed upstairs with them to his room, and they looked for it on his map but could not find it. Then he got out other maps that were even older, and they kept on looking until they finally located the castle. However, it was thousands of miles away.

"How will I ever get there?" asked the man.

"I've got two hours to spare," said the giant. "I'll carry you as far as I can, but then I must return home and nurse our child." So he carried the man until he was about a hundred hours' walk from the castle and said, "You can go the rest of the way by yourself."[3]

The household of the giants is unlike any other I know. Here we have two giant brothers, raising a child. It is the kind of household you might expect to turn up in a Coen brothers movie. Finding the hidden story in any fairy tale starts with asking questions. How did the two giants come by this child? Did they find the child on the doorstep or in a basket floating down the river? What would it be like for two giants who know nothing about parenting to suddenly find themselves responsible for an infant? And how old is this child? Is it a boy or a girl? Is the child a giant or a changeling from the human world? Where is the child's mother? Did the giants devour her? They seem too good-hearted for that.

If giants are not your cup of tea, you can look at the scene from the child's point of view. What would it be like for a child to lose its mother and father and be brought up by two huge beings in a magic house in the middle of the forest?

For magic the house surely is, though the storyteller does not once use that word. From the outside, the house looks small because the giant standing in front of it looks so big. But Alice's fall down the rabbit hole has taught us never to judge the size of a space by its entrance. The interior of the house must be the right size for the giants, for we do not see them ducking under doorways or bumping their heads on the ceiling. Indeed, the house is spacious enough for each giant to have his own room, apparently on different floors. They also have enough closet space to stash their map collection—a feature many of us would envy—and enough spare rooms to archive the oldest maps. Leafing back through the maps, they seem to be going backward in time, the way a fossil hunter does when he or she reads the rocks back to the moment when the mountain was as powerless as a new tooth breaking through the thin crust of the earth. The story hidden in "The Raven" is rooted in characters who live in the magic space that weaves clock time and time out of mind into a seamless fabric. Anyone who has ever looked at a map of the sky knows that what we love about maps is the illusion that we can measure infinity.

But the hidden story in a fairy tale does not always arrive complete with giants, a child, and a magic house. Sometimes a single image is all you are given. Take, for example, another Grimm fairy tale, "Faithful Ferdinand and Unfaithful Ferdinand." The hero, Faithful Ferdinand, is sent on a dangerous journey by the king to fetch his beloved princess from a country inhabited by giants less kindly than the two cartographers with the baby. But luck follows the hero. His horse instructs him to throw the giants a few slabs of meat and they'll help him. "Just take a few of them with you and go up into the castle, where you'll find the princess lying asleep, but you mustn't wake her." The giants carry the princess in her bed directly to the king. And now you expect me to say, "So they married and lived happily ever after." But wait—not so fast. The princess's mode of arrival did not give her time to pack. Now, what would a princess pack? Beautiful gowns? Jewels? Surely a servant could be sent to fetch these. Here's the sentence that opens the door to the hidden story:

"When she [the princess] arrived at the king's palace, she told him that she could not live without her private papers that were still in her castle."

A princess whose papers are more important to her than her marriage to the king? What on earth is in them? Why such secrecy and why such urgency? Is she writing a novel? Keeping a diary? Is she doing her accounts and cooking the books? Conducting scientific experiments? Has she discovered the square root of love?

Ferdinand braves the giants once more and the storyteller makes much of how the papers are retrieved. "When they reached the castle, the horse told Faithful Ferdinand to go into the

39

princess's bedroom, where he would find the papers lying on the table. So he went in and got them. . . . Afterward Faithful Ferdinand brought the papers to the palace, where the wedding was then held."[4]

And thereby hangs a tale. The reader or listener is never told what those papers contain. That is for the writer to decide. The princess has her own story to tell. A minor character in Ferdinand's story, a major character in her own, with a supporting cast of eccentrics, villains, and heroes.

If you write it, they will come.

NOTES

1. *Everyman and Medieval Miracle Plays,* A. C. Cawley, ed. (New York: Dutton, 1959), pp. 43–44.

2. Henry James, "The Art of Fiction," *The Art of Fiction and Other Essays* (New York: Oxford University Press, 1948), p. 11.

3. "The Raven," *The Complete Fairy Tales of the Brothers Grimm,* Jack Zipes, trans. (New York: Bantam Books, 2002), p. 317.

4. "Faithful Ferdinand and Unfaithful Ferdinand," *The Complete Fairy Tales of the Brothers Grimm,* Jack Zipes, trans. (New York: Bantam Books, 2002), pp. 413, 414.

The Muse Goes Greyhound

To make a prairie it takes a clover and one bee,
One clover, and a bee,
And revery.
The revery alone will do,
If bees are few.

——EMILY DICKINSON[1]

No BEES, NO CLOVER? This is no ordinary reverie. This is the power of the imagination to praise the living and raise the dead. This is inspiration. The person who first taught me the meaning of that word was not a poet but a storyteller, and that storyteller was my mother.

Not long after I turned seven my mother decided to give me a Hallowe'en party. She never did anything by halves. When she called us for dinner on Christmas Eve, you knew the plum pudding would be spectacular. She'd turn off the lights in the dining room, ignite the pudding sauce, and make her entrance. Her preparations for any great event were always conducted in secret. She told me she was going shopping for paper streamers, black cats, and witch's hats to hang in the windows. She did not mention a brief trip to the butcher shop, nor did she allude to her purchases: two oysters, a kidney, and a liver. I wanted to bob for apples as they floated in a tub of water, but Mother felt this was unhygienic. She agreed to make a devil's food cake for my seven guests.

I suppose we ate the devil's food cake but I have no memory of it. The only part of the day I can recall with absolute clarity is my mother's storytelling. She gathered us around her in the living room, pulled the drapes, and turned off the lights. The room, which had only one small window, was eclipsed; we could not see each other's faces.

The giggling subsided, and out of the darkness my mother's voice unwound her story.

"You think I am the kindly Mrs. Willard," it murmured, "don't you?"

Everyone grew very quiet. The silence was so profound that even I had a twinge of doubt.

"Now I'll tell you the truth. I am a murderess. And yesterday afternoon I killed a man and hid his body under the attic stairs."

I was sure this could not be true. My mother had said she was going shopping, and here were the decorations to prove it. And she hadn't even been gone that long.

"You don't believe me? Put forth your hands."

Seven pairs of hands were extended, slowly. We nudged them together like petals on a night-loving flower. My mother spoke very slowly now, as if she were afraid of her own words.

"Here are his eyes. Blue they were, and very beautiful."

Into my hands slid two small slippery objects. The shock of this unraveled my courage. I shrieked and threw them into the hands of the child to my left, who also shrieked. Soon everyone in the room except, of course, my mother was screaming, our hands outstretched as we pawed the air toward each other.

Did my mother wait for us to calm down? No. Over the din she shouted,

"And here is his liver!"

The organ that dropped into my hands felt huge and slipper-shaped. My mother did not dwell on the lurid details of the victim's death but on his life and her motives for taking it. It was not the damp weight of the liver but the matter-of-fact details in her story that for a few seconds convinced me something terrible really had happened in our house. The liver slid off my palm into the hands of a child whose face I could not see.

"And here, my dears, is his heart, which I cut still beating from his breast—"

A howl of such pure terror rose from one of the children that my mother called for lights. Since none of the guests could find the switch, she stumbled to her feet and groped her way to the nearest lamp. A comforting click—and light gave us back our faces. But the sight of seven children and one confessed murderer, all of us with bloodied hands, was no comfort to the little girl seated on the coffee table, quaking so hard that her patent leather shoes could be heard tapping against the glass top.

Parents were called, hands were washed, coats gathered up. The father of the little girl whose howl had ended the party telephoned the next morning. He'd had to give his child a sleeping pill to calm her down, and he demanded an explanation.

"I got inspired," said my mother.

Every description of inspiration I've read since that day tells me she was speaking the truth. Plato might have been describing my mother when he wrote that "all good poets . . . are inspired and possessed. . . . [T]here is no invention in him until he has been inspired and is out of his senses."[2]

An exaggeration, perhaps? I think not. Writers who have been lucky enough to compose a splendid work in a burst of inspiration agree on one thing: the gift seems to come from outside "a nameless storm, a hurricane in the spirit . . . , all that was fiber in me and fabric cracked—eating was not to be thought of, God knows who fed me."[3] Rilke was also writing the *Sonnets to Orpheus* during this period. The fifty-six poems in that collection were, he observed, the "most enigmatic dictation I have ever held through and achieved; the whole first part was written down in a single breathless act of obedience, between the 2nd and 5th of February, without one word being doubtful or having to be changed."[4]

But inspiration—that sense of the story or poem dictating itself—need not arrive in a whirlwind. We know from our own experience how reverie, or what Whitman called loafing and inviting your soul, can unexpectedly put the poem or story into motion. Lewis Carroll's account of how he composed *Alice in Wonderland* shows inspiration arriving as quietly as a dream. Picture Charles Dodgson and his colleague from Oxford, and the three young daughters of the dean of Christ Church, taking their ease on the most peaceful of boating expeditions. Dodgson is rowing. The weather is warm on this fourth day of July, and the children beg for a story.

Later Dodgson confessed that "in a desperate attempt to strike out some new line of fairy-lore" he sent his heroine straight down a rabbit hole "without the least idea what was to happen afterwards." His colleague, impressed by the tale as it unfolded, inquired whether this was an "extempore romance. "Yes," replied Dodgson, "I'm inventing as we go along."[5]

Did the regular rhythmic stroke of the oars help to set Dodgson's mind free? In her book, *Becoming a Writer,* Dorthea Brande examines the rituals writers have used to bring on the state of inspiration, and a regular, rhythmic activity—walking, knitting, whittling—is common to many of them. Such activity, she suggests, puts the writer into a sort of waking dream. And you needn't be Charles Dodgson or Rilke to experience this. Every author, she claims, "in some way which he has come on by luck or long search, puts himself into a very light state of hypnosis. The attention is held, but *just* held; there is no serious demand on it. Far behind the mind's surface, so deep that he is seldom aware . . . that any activity is going forward, his story is being fused and welded into an integrated work."[6]

Several years ago I had the pleasure of reviewing a book called *Darkangel,* the first novel of a talented young writer, Meredith Pierce. The novel is a fantasy, set on the moon. What struck me as I read the first chapter were her vivid images of a world as strange as the bottom of the sea and as particular as my own garden. Here is Meredith Pierce's moonscape, as one of her characters sees it:

She fell to watching the landscape, the lie of the rocks. She listened to the bell-thorn, silvery thin briars that tinkled like glass in the rare mountain wind. She watched the small, rose-colored lizards sunning themselves in the last hours of Solstar before crawling into their crags again to sleep for another long night-shade. She looked at the petrified bones in the rocks, bones of fishes, eels, and water plants left over from the time when the steeps had been nothing but flat mud bottom, and all the world a sea.[7]

How did the author arrive at such a place? She had just read Carl Jung's autobiography, *Memories, Dreams, Reflections,* and taken notice of the elaborate fantasy of one of Jung's patients, who was convinced she had lived on the moon. The moon people were in danger of extinction: on the mountains of the moon there lived a vampire who kidnapped and killed women and children. But how on earth did the patient's fantasy give Meredith Pierce the voice and plot of her novel? During the long bus ride on her way home from a writers' conference, she found herself mulling over the image of the lunar vampire. Presently the theme, plot, and shape of the novel came to her "all of a piece" in what she has called a waking dream-vision, to which the long bus ride made her especially receptive. When you travel by Greyhound, you never know when the muse will take the seat next to you. Writers who speak of being inspired have learned to treasure these images whose power they don't fully understand and that arrive with their own laws and their own logic.

For anyone who would like to believe that all good writing comes from inspiration, it is a humbling experience to look at "A Christmas Carol," published in facsimile by the Morgan Library. Every writer should frame his opening page and hang it over his or her desk, for it shows what Dickens himself called "the story-weaver at his loom." The page is so crossed out and written over that one can hardly find the first sentence, which sounds so right and inevitable: "Marley was dead to begin with, there is no doubt whatever about that." To one of his sons, Dickens wrote, "Look at such of my manuscripts as are in the library . . . and think of the patient hours devoted year after year to single lines."[8]

Few of us have the discipline of Anthony Trollope, who kept a diary, divided into weeks, while he worked on a book. Each day he recorded the number of pages he'd written, so idleness seemed to stare him in the face. The truth is, all of us have days when we seem to accomplish nothing. "Dawdly days," John Steinbeck called them, noting that the dawdly days seemed to alternate with the days in which he wrote well. "The crazy thing is," he added, "that I get about the same number of words down either way."[9]

Discipline and inspiration sound like two countries with an ocean between them. But are they so far apart? Can the hard work of revision end in inspiration? It took Lewis Carroll seven months to revise the story of Alice's adventures down the rabbit hole that came to him so artlessly that afternoon in July, and he proved to himself that revision can be as full of surprises as the original piece. "In writing it out," he said, "I added many fresh ideas, which seemed to grow of themselves upon the original stock; and many more added themselves when, years afterwards, I wrote it all over again for publication . . . Sometimes an idea comes at night, when I have had to get up and strike a light to note it down . . . but whenever or however it comes, *it comes of itself* . . . 'Alice' and the 'Looking Glass' are made up almost wholly of bits and scraps, single ideas which came of themselves."[10]

We know that the muse is most attracted to those who know the secret of actively waiting for the right word, the right image. Gathering the pieces and finding the poem or story hidden there is a little like working on a puzzle that looks simple on the surface but hides its own peculiar difficulties. Several months ago I was browsing at a flea market and came across a pile of old jigsaw puzzles. Knowing my husband's fondness for such things, I rummaged through the lot. A few had the finished picture on the cover, conventional paintings of horses, steamboats, kittens, and the Eiffel Tower. Suddenly one box caught my eye. It was carefully tied with string, like the plain boxes in which my mother would carry a cake she'd bought at the bakery. On the lid was an inscription:

Supreme Picture Puzzle With the Interlocking Feature. Over 200 pieces.

Shakespeare at the Court of Elizabeth. One piece missing.

The subject sounded promising, and I admired the honesty of the seller who was willing to reveal the flaw in his product. I turned the box over to see the painting of Queen Bess and her courtiers but found none. The old man behind the counter watched me with disdain.

"You don't want that one. That's for serious puzzle-lovers."

"No, it's not," I said. "It's only got two hundred pieces. If I had the picture, I could do this in a couple of hours."

"Professionals never use a picture," he said. "Doing a puzzle with a picture is like painting by number."

I bought the puzzle, and after supper Eric and I poured the pieces out on the dining room table. We started with the edge pieces, which gave us the dimensions of the puzzle. Soon we realized it would be small like a story, not vast like a novel. This puzzle was finicky. It would take its own sweet time—and ours—before it showed us the characters, the scenes, the action hidden in those pieces.

We started eating dinner in the kitchen.

We stopped entertaining.

We sat at the dining room table for hours, matching colors and shapes, muttering, "This goes with that, this fits there." Sometimes a face emerged, but whose? Or a man's leg appeared, but doing what? I couldn't walk through the dining room without lingering over those pieces, turning them, trying them here or here or there, till I found what worked.

Not so different, I thought, from writing a novel or a poem. When I'm writing a poem, it is comforting to have the edge pieces, the shape and the sound of the thing. That's the value of exercises in a workshop; the exercise gives you a formal element that frees you to take the first step. When the novelist Marguerite Young was teaching at the New School, one of her first assignments was surely useful for both poets and fiction writers: write a three-page sentence, logical as to grammatical structure—musical as to phrasing, imagistic . . . rather than vague. . . . To make this sentence move, the writer is forced to observe and weave into it all the fleeting, apparently discrepant thoughts which do not usually fall into short, staccato sentences . . . I call this . . . the dragnet sentence—the students are like fishermen dragging the waters with the net and bringing in whatever haul there is.

She cautioned her students that between the great writer and the unrealized writer, "there may be only this difference—that the latter has a very active toll keeper, turning many things back, as he is fearful of writing what he really thinks and feels."[11]

Freedom from fear. When I sit down to write a story, I have to give myself permission not to write the events chronologically. The still small voice of the muse whispers, ""If you write the scenes you want to write, regardless of where they belong, the story itself may give you a far more original arrangement than the logical one you started with." Or when I'm writing a poem: "Shake up the order of the stanzas."

And I do, just to let the muse know I'm listening.

I envy writers who have had the good fortune to be brought up in an oral tradition. They have been listening for shape and sound since they were born. Several years ago the college at which I teach was fortunate to have as its writer-in-residence David Yali-Manisi, a poet from South Africa, who was the official praise singer for his village. As praise singer, it was his job to compose poems that commemorated important events. To most of us, the circumstances under which he composed these poems would be a nightmare. Imagine that the entire faculty and student body of the college has gathered in a great hall. With nothing written and nothing planned, the poet arrives to speak his new poem. Someone from the audiovisual department adjusts the tape recorder.

The poet explains that he can't get started unless he holds something in his hand to help him beat out the rhythm, preferably a spear. Nobody in the audience has a spear. Somebody offers

48

him a cane, and with this in his hand he turns to the audience, and in a voice quite unlike his regular one he chants a poem about his visit to this campus, a poem that has a clear sense of form and rhythm and that he is making up as he goes along, before hundreds of witnesses.

When he has finished, he cannot remember what he has said, and he listens to the tape with genuine curiosity. Since the poem is in his own language, which few in the room understand, he translates it for us.

Afterwards a student asks him, "Don't you get stage fright?"

"What is stage fright?" asks the poet.

"Stage fright is when you stand up, and suddenly you have nothing to say."

"If I had nothing to say, I wouldn't stand up," replies the poet in a puzzled voice.

After many conversations with Mr. Manisi, I understood why this was easier for him than it would be for most of us.

"Ever since I was a child, I heard poetry, I heard the songs of my people. I knew the forms and the phrases by heart. When I was sent to take care of the cattle, I made up songs for them. There was no separate place for poetry. It was all around us."

Though few of us come to writing with such an unbroken experience of poetry, a writer engaged in actively waiting for the story or poem to emerge has something in common with the Ojibway boy or girl sent to the woods without food, to fast and await the gift of a vision or song from a guardian spirit. What the writer awaits, of course, is inspiration. And immersing yourself in your work is still one of the best ways to find it.

But what happens if the muse doesn't show up?

I think there are two kinds of blocks for writers. The first is temporary: in the middle of a story or a poem, you lose your way. You can no longer hear the voice of your story, the music of your poem. Here is Charles Dickens describing the agony of writing on a day when the muse has to be coaxed:

"I am in a hideous state of mind in which I walk down the stairs every five minutes, look out of the window once in two. . . . I am steeped in my story, and rise and fall by turns into enthusiasm and depression."[12]

Some writers find that nothing breaks up the mental logjam better than a good nap, a method that worked for Thomas Edison, who found that solutions to problems often came to him in his sleep. Other writers take long walks. Dickens is said to have walked fifteen or twenty miles in one day while he was working on "A Christmas Carol."

The second kind of block is more serious. You have an idea for a book you've been carrying in your heard for months, even years, but that idea has closed itself up like a cottage shuttered and locked for the winter, and you have no idea where the muse has hidden the key. No amount of walking or napping will help you find it, for like the castle of the sleeping princess in the fairy tale, time itself is the spell-breaker here, as Kafka acknowledged when he observed that an artist's material "must be worked on by the spirit"[13] and will open the door when it is ready to be found. You can be certain that from its hiding place, it watches as you sweep the steps and keep the path clear for its coming.

Perhaps the gap between discipline and inspiration is not so great after all. Most of the time, the shaping and honing take place by the harsh light of day, under the fierce eye of the writer. But once in a while the shaping and honing seem to happen out of sight, and what arrives shines with the strange truth of its dark origins. A woman sitting in the dark surrounded by children tells a terrifying story. She did not set out to terrify, only to amuse; she does not know what possessed her. When Saul Bellow observed that you never have to change anything you get up to write down in the middle of the night, he was acknowledging that in the cocoon of forgetting, what was born clumsy is given wings.

NOTES

1. Emily Dickinson, "To make a prairie," *The Complete Poems of Emily Dickinson,* Thomas H. Johnson, ed. (Boston: Little, Brown, 1960), p. 710.

2. "Ion," *The Dialogues of Plato,* B. Jowett, trans. (New York: Random House, 1892), p. 289.

3. *Letters of Rainer Maria Rilke, 1910–1929* Jane Bannard Greene and M. D. Herter Norton, trans. (New York: W.W. Norton, 1948), p. 290.

4. Rainer Maria Rilke, quoted in "Foreword," M. D. Herter Norton, *Sonnets to Orpheus* (New York: Norton, 1942), p. 7.

5. Derek Hudson, *Lewis Carroll* (London: Constable, 1954), 128.

6. Dorothea Brande, *Becoming a Writer* (Los Angeles: J. P. Tarcher, 1981), p. 160.

7. Meredith Pierce, *The Darkangel* (Boston: Little Brown, Atlantic Monthly Press, 1982), p. 9.

8. John Mortimer, "Poorhouses, Pamphlets and Marley's Ghost," *New York Times,* December 24, 1993, p. A27.

9. Susan Shaughnessy, *Walking on Alligators: A Book of Meditations for Writers* (San Francisco: HarperSan Francisco, 1993), p. 117.

10. "'Alice' on the Stage," *The Lewis Carroll Picture Book,* ed. Stuart Dodgson Collingwood, ed. (London: T. Fisher Unwin, 1899), 166–67.

11. Marguerite Young, "Inviting the Muses," *Mademoiselle,* September 1965, p. 231.

12. Mortimer, "Poorhouses, Pamphlets and Marley's Ghost."

13. Gustav Janouch, *Conversations with Kafka: Notes and Reminiscences* (New York: Praeger, 1953), p. 88.

The Friendship Tarot

I lay out the cards of our friendship.

The Child

The card shows a child with chocolate on his face wandering through an art gallery in downtown Poughkeepsie devoted—for two weeks—to illustrations from children's books. Ilse Vogel and I have not met, but we both have work in this show. In one room stands the six-foot doll's house I made when I was writing *A Visit to William Blake's Inn*. In the next room hang Ilse's meticulous pen-and-ink drawings for her book, *Dodo Every Day*.

What I saw: an elegant woman with white hair, a knitted cloche, and eyes that missed nothing.

What she saw: a woman with a seven-year-old boy whose face was smeared with chocolate.

What I thought: Who is this remarkable person?

What Ilse thought: Her child has a dirty face, but does she worry about it? No. And neither does the child.

The Garden

The card shows two married couples eating dinner in a garden: Eric and me, Howard and Ilse. Four artists: one painter (Howard), one photographer (Eric), one writer (me), and Ilse, who can't be pinned down to one category since she illustrates her own stories. The dinner Ilse has prepared is exquisite. Butter blooms in a little pot; Ilse has sculpted it into the face of a sunflower. Howard helps her carry dishes from the tiny kitchen into the Francesca, a shelter shingled in nasturtiums and morning glories. The front is entirely open to view; over the edge of the second story dangle the tails of four sleeping cats. Once it was a rickety outbuilding for storing tools. Now it is paved with round river stones chosen and put into place years ago by Ilse. Shortly after she'd laid the last stone, she felt chest pains. The day she came home from the hospital, Howard filled the house with anemones.

Ilse heaps seconds on our plates without asking us and tells us they bought this small white house in the country because they loved the apple tree blooming outside the kitchen window. The soil is rocky but the garden is full of flowers; Ilse has put out one hundred and four pots of flowers. When a large tabby springs from behind one of them, Ilse explains that they are down to ten cats.

"Ten cats!" exclaims Eric.

"We have only two," I add apologetically.

Is this the first step into friendship? Ilse knows right away she can discuss the excellence of cats without boring me: Velvet Paws, Parsley, Comedy Cat, Mr. Goldie, Chives. Summer and winter the ten cats that live with Howard and Ilse sleep in the garage at night.

Winter and summer the two cats that live with Eric and me sleep at the foot of our bed so they can watch over us.

The Journey

The card shows three people in a car headed for New York. Ilse wears the same knitted cloche she wore at the gallery, and Howard's hat is the identical shade of oatmeal. When I remark on this, Ilse explains that she knitted them both.

We three are traveling to New York to see *The Tin Drum*. On the way, Ilse explains that she lived in Berlin all during the war, so naturally she's curious to see this film.

Of the movie I remember only a few scenes, not because the film was forgettable but because of what happened on the trip back.

The Story

The card shows a woman talking and a woman listening.

I am riding in the back seat of the car and I lean forward and ask, "Ilse, was it really like that in Germany?"

Ilse answers by telling me about the day the Russians marched into Berlin.

"When the Russians came so close to the house, you could hear them talking and shouting. And all the inhabitants of the house were sitting in the bunkers except me, because I hated to be down there with the Nazis. I was in my apartment with a friend of mine. And then we heard shooting and voices, and then we heard a sound as if masses and masses of water would come rushing in, and then my friend said, 'Oh, something has hit the canister of gasoline,' and within seconds I saw the flames and the gasoline floating in under the doorway of my apartment, and everything was in flames. There was just one window where we could get out. We crossed the yard to the door of the bunker and went inside and then the house did burn with tremendous speed. Smoke came and people started to pray and to sing, and others cursed and screamed. I sat with my friend and we held hands and I said, 'This is the end, there's no way out.' And my friend had a little flute with him which he always carried. I'll show it to you tomorrow—I still have it. He pulled it out and played a little Bach sonata for us, to comfort us."

She tells me how she worked in the Resistance against Hitler, hiding Jews in her apartment and printing passports to smuggle them out of Germany. Two hours later we are back in Pough-keepsie.

"Ilse," I say, "have you written this down?"

"It's not a story for children," she says. "And I can't find the right voice to tell it."

"You must tell it," I say, "so people don't forget." Ilse asks to use the bathroom. When she emerges she says with a smile, "I'm so glad your house isn't neat all the time."

The Gift

The card shows a restaurant strung with red and green lights.

The week before Christmas, Ilse and Howard and Eric and I meet for lunch at Dickens. Ilse calls ahead so that we can have the same table we had last year—a table intended for six. She tells the waitress we are expecting another person, a man, and during the meal she laments his bad manners—why couldn't he have phoned? She brings the snapshots we took of each other last year. In the snapshots we are always opening presents. Here I am, opening the present Ilse made for me: a muff, to keep my hands warm. It is made of brown corduroy, lined with synthetic lamb's wool, and decorated in orange and turquoise and lavender braid, felt hearts, pyramids, and silver beads, each bead no bigger than a mustard seed. It has a corduroy strap and a pocket, into which Ilse has tucked a bright red handkerchief.

Since I ride a bicycle to class and my arms are usually full of books, I seldom have the leisure to use a muff unless I decide to take a muff-walk: a walk with no other purpose than exercise and pleasure. Which is probably why Ilse gave it to me.

This year Howard gives Eric a book of Vuillard's paintings and Ilse gives me a Waring handheld blender that she assures me will make cooking much easier.

Eric gives Howard a photograph he took inside the conservatory of the New York Botanical Gardens, and I give Ilse a set of flannel sheets and pillowcases printed with cats.

Food

The card shows dinner tables, side by side.

When we eat dinner at their house, they serve hors d'oeuvres and drinks in the living room or the garden, just for the four of us. Ilse makes the salad dressing. The courses arrive in succession at the proper time.

When they eat dinner at ours, I am famished from having skipped lunch to meet with students, and I rush everything to the table at once. The salad dressing is Paul Newman's finest, the cake is the handiwork of the Aurora Café Bakery. The last time I baked a cake, it collapsed like an old hat and I filled in the holes and cracks with frosting, which made it astonishingly heavy but quite tasty. Howard warned Ilse not to eat it.

"All that chocolate is bad for your heart," he said softly.

She smiled and took another bite.

The Moon

The card shows four people perched on top of the world.

Ilse phones us in great excitement. Tonight, if we stand on a certain hill a mile from their house, we can watch the sun go down and the moon come up, all at the same time. She has checked the weather; the sky will be clear.

The road to the hill runs past stables and pastures broken by white fencing into parcels that give expensive horses enough room to run free by keeping them apart from each other. Howard regrets that the landscape feels so owned.

When we climb out of the car and look east and west from the crest of the windy hill, the valley sweeps broadly around us; could we see the Hudson if we knew where to find it?

As the sun slides into its nest of light behind the Catskills, the moon rises silently, secretly. She is so pale and thin that she might be the shed carapace of some large round animal. As darkness gathers, she grows solider, more golden.

"In German, the moon is masculine," says Ilse. "And the sun is feminine."

I can't think of another language in which those genders are assigned to my old friends in the sky.

Ilse says she is trying to write about those last days before the fall of Berlin, but she is not yet ready to read me what she has written.

The Bird

The card shows an empty cage in a garden.

Ilse phones us—can we come over and see the dove? It seems that the postmistress in their little town of Bangall runs an animal adoption service on the side, and she has presented Ilse with a dove.

When we arrived, Ilse has put its cage on a pile of stones in the garden, like an altar to flight. The cage is made of the sticks that Ilse gathered in the yard, but it is very small, and when Eric and I approach, the dove beats her wings against the bars. All during dinner she makes endearing noises.

"You can't imagine how we enjoy hearing that wonderful sound," says Ilse. "And the cats don't seem to notice her."

We sit outside and watch the singular stars arrive, one by one, like notes in a music box winding down to silence.

The next day I telephone Joanne, a friend of mine who does excellent carpentry, and ask her to make a catproof cage for Ilse's dove. I tell her it should be made of sticks gathered in a forest and it should be huge. Ilse's birthday is two weeks away—could she possibly have it finished by then?

Two weeks later, Joanne drives up with a cage nearly as tall as herself on her truck. It is a gazebo, a minaret, a chapel, it is the mother of all birdcages. I phone Howard and tell him we want to deliver it as a surprise to Ilse, who likes surprises but does not like unexpected visitors. Howard can tell her whatever he likes; we will arrive with the cage at eleven o'clock on Thursday.

When we appear, the two of them are sitting in the garden, attended by Velvet Paws. Joanne and I carry the cage across the lawn. Ilse is speechless with astonishment. This is just the way I hoped she would be.

"You've given me exactly what I wanted!" she exclaims.

The dove takes to the cage at once. Soon it no longer feels like a cage; Ilse adds branches and leaves and nasturtiums and she removes the bottom so that the dove sits directly on the grass. How good the grass feels on her little coral feet! All night long she enjoys dewfall and moonrise and starshine. When the sun warms the dark world, Howard arrives with her breakfast.

One morning Howard goes to feed the dove and finds a dash of bloody feathers. There is a snake in Eden; nothing but a snake could insinuate itself into so stout a cage.

Ilse mourns her dove. All winter the cage is filled only with cream-colored twigs and the curious seedpods that catch her eye in the garden. One day the postmistress telephones her. A relative of the slain dove has recently laid a clutch of eggs; two of them hatched. Would Ilse like two doves? Howard snakeproofs the cage. It is spring again and the voices of Ilse's doves are heard in the land.

Death

The card shows a shelf on which Ilse has arranged the skulls of their cats. After their deaths, she digs them up. The skulls are light and beautiful as parchment.

"Some people think it's a strange thing to do," she says, "but see how beautiful their bones are!"

When I cook chicken, I save not only the wishbone but the breastbone. Scrubbed clean and dried, the breastbone looks like a mask or a saddle intended for an animal unaccustomed to carrying passengers. On the apple tree in our back yard hang the shells of half a dozen horseshoe crabs I found on Cape Cod. Anyone passing the tree would take it for the site of a secret ceremony devoted to saving what holds us up but is never seen under the living flesh.

The Book

The card shows pages falling and gathering like snow.

Ilse is now seriously at work on her stories about life in Germany under Hitler. Howard is typing them for her. The stories arrive in the mail, one by one, in white envelopes bordered with a green stripe.

Without telling her, I am sending them to my editor at Harcourt Brace.

Velvet Paws has had her kittens behind a canvas of Howard's that he imprudently left leaning against an upstairs wall. Ilse invites us to view the kittens. Eric and I sit in the living room of the little white house and wait for the great moment. We wait and wait. And suddenly here is Ilse, presenting them to us in a basket lined with violets and strawberry leaves, as if she had just picked them in the garden.

Later, as we are leafing through a box of old photographs, I pull out a picture of two blond girls standing side by side: Ilse and her twin sister, Erika, who died of diphtheria when they were nine.

"Which one is you?" I ask.

Ilse is not sure.

"Perhaps that one, with the knees bent a little. Erika was born first and she always was the more courageous one."

Eight years ago, when I published my first novel, *Things Invisible to See,* I dedicated it to Ilse and Howard.

Today I open the book of Ilse's stories, *Bad Times, Good Friends,* and find it is dedicated to Eric and me. Over the dedication is Ilse's pen-and-ink drawing of a dove turning into a woman. She is flying over a bed of pansies, carrying three tulips in one hand and pointing to our names with the other.

"They didn't want a dove-woman on the dedication page," says Ilse. "I had to fight for it."

A Wand Made of Words:
The Litany Poem

❦

LET ME START BY explaining what the litany, as a poetic form, is not. It is not a liturgical prayer in which phrases are sung or chanted by a leader alternating with phrases sung or chanted in response by the congregation. As a poetic form, the litany can be described as an incantatory recitation built on a simple word pattern: every line, or nearly every line, starts with the same word.

The simplest litany I know appears in the picture book *Goodnight Moon,* though many other picture book texts make use of this form because it is so versatile.

> Goodnight comb
> Goodnight brush
> Goodnight nobody
> Goodnight mush
> And goodnight to the old lady whispering "hush"[1]

When I teach the litany form to my students, I begin with two traditional poems that are still tied to their magical and liturgical origins. The first is Psalm 150. Joyful and impersonal, it opens with the following lines:

> Praise the Lord!
> Praise God in his sanctuary;
>   praise him in his mighty firmament!

Praise him for his mighty deeds;
    praise him according to his ex-
        ceeding greatness!

Praise him with trumpet sound;
    praise him with lute and harp!
Praise him with timbrel and dance;
    praise him with strings and pipe!
Praise him with sounding cymbals;
    praise him with loud clanging
        cymbals!
Let everything that breathes praise
    the Lord!
Praise the Lord![2]

The poet who uses the litany form to praise more secular plea-
sures finds that it allows for great expansiveness within the ele-
gance of its formulaic opening. In "Song of Myself," Whitman's
long lines give momentum to a catalogue of people seen both as
individuals and studies for a genre painting:

. . . .
The pilot seizes the king-pin, he heaves down with a strong arm,
The mate stands braced in the whale-boat, lance and harpoon are
    ready,
The duck-shooter walks by silent and cautious stretches,
The deacons are ordain'd with cross'd hands at the altar,
The spinning-girl retreats and advances to the hum of the big
    wheel,
. . . .[3]

A poem written as a single sentence can break out of the catalogue structure. In Linda Pastan's "Because," nearly every line is a
dependent clause and the poem moves with the speed and sus-
pense of a well-wrought narrative.

BECAUSE

Because the night you asked me,
the small scar of the quarter moon

61

had healed—the moon was whole again;
because life seemed so short;
because life stretched before me
like the darkened halls of nightmare;
because I knew exactly what I wanted;
because I knew exactly nothing;
because I shed my childhood with my clothes—
they both had years of wear left in them;
because your eyes were darker than my father's;
because my father said I could do better;
because I wanted badly to say no;
because Stanley Kowalski shouted "Stella . . .";
because you were a door I could slam shut;
because endings are written before beginnings;
because I knew that after twenty years
you'd bring the plants inside for winter
and make a jungle we'd sleep in naked;
because I had free will;
because everything is ordained;
I said yes.[4]

Remove the formulaic opening from these lines, and the poem transforms itself into a narrative about a young woman's indecision. The litany form puts distance between the reader and the speaker and turns the story into a meditation on a larger theme: the paradox of our ability to want what we do not want and to desire opposites.

Why are poems in this form so seductive? Why do readers who loathe cats read even a short passage from Christopher Smart's meditation on his cat Jeoffry with grudging admiration and genuine delight?

For I will consider my Cat Jeoffry.
For he is the servant of the Living God duly and daily serving him.
For at the first glance of the glory of God in the East he worships in his way.
For this is done by wreathing his body seven times round with elegant quickness.[5]

Isn't it because the litany can amuse and astonish us without baffling us, a quality it shares with dreams? Like dreams it explains nothing, even while it buries the connections between images whose significance is so private as to be unfathomable on a first reading. An excerpt from Mark Strand's "From a Litany" demonstrates this tension between the personal statements and the public voice:

> I praise the secrecy of doors, the openness of windows.
> I praise the depth of closets,
> I praise the wind, the rising generations of air.
> I praise the trees on whose branches shall sit the Cock of
>   Portugal and the Polish Cock.
> I praise the palm trees of Rio and those that shall grow in
>   London.
> I praise the gardeners, the worms and the small plants that
>   praise each other.
> I praise the sweet berries of Georgetown, Maine and the
>   song of the white-throated sparrow.[6]

The second example of a traditional litany poem that I give my students is "The Killer," a Cherokee curse that is still rooted in its shamanistic origins. I give the entire text as it appears in Jerome Rothenberg's *Technicians of the Sacred:*

THE KILLER

Careful:	my knife drills your soul
	listen, whatever-your-name-is
	One of the wolf people
listen	I'll grind your saliva into the earth
listen	I'll cover your bones with black flint
listen	" " " " " feathers
listen	" " " " " rocks
Because	you're going out where it's empty
	Black coffin on the hill
listen	the black earth will hide you, will
	find you a black hut
	Out where it's dark, in that country
listen	I'm bringing a box for your bones

```
                    A black box
                    A grave with black pebbles
        listen      your soul's spilling out
        listen      it's blue
```
(Cherokee Indian)[7]

The reason for the imperative in traditional litanies is obvious: the speaker is singing or chanting to a particular audience, whether a whole congregation or a single malevolent spirit. But when Whitman uses it near the end of "Starting from Paumanok," he is addressing a more general audience of readers known and unknown, present and future, and his repetition of "See" at the beginning of each line in poem #18 gives the poem an urgency it would not otherwise have:

> See, steamers steaming through my poems,
> See, in my poems immigrants continually coming and landing[8]

When the formulaic verb is *let,* as in Denise Levertov's "Psalm Concerning the Castle," the imperative is directed at fate, which may or may not be listening, and therefore to mortal ears sounds like a wish, or even a blessing. I was lucky enough to hear her read this poem and describe its origin: the contemplation of a painting so intense that it became an image of harmony in the soul.

> Let me be at the place of the castle.
> Let the castle be within me.
> Let it rise foursquare from the moat's ring.
> Let the moat's waters reflect green plumage of ducks, let the shells of swimming turtles break the surface or be seen through the rippling depths.
> Let horsemen be stationed at the rim of it, and a dog, always alert on the brink of sleep.
> Let the space under the first storey be dark, let the water lap the stone posts, and vivid green slime glimmer upon them; let a boat be kept there.
> Let the caryatids of the second storey be bears upheld on beams that are dragons.

On the parapet of the central room, let there be four archers,
   looking off to the four horizons. Within, let the prince be at
   home, let him sit in deep thought, at peace, all the windows
   open to the loggias.
Let the young queen sit above, in the cool air, her child in
   her arms; let her look with joy at the great circle, the
   pilgrim shadows, the work of the sun and the play of
   the wind. Let her walk to and fro. Let the columns
   uphold the roof, let the storeys uphold the columns,
   let there be dark space below the lowest floor, let the
   castle rise foursquare out of the moat, let the moat be a
   ring and the water deep, let the guardians guard it, let
   there be wide lands around it, let that country where it
   stands within me, let me be where it is.[9]

The images are ordered as the eye would see them, starting at
the bottom of the painting and slowly raising one's gaze to the
roof and to the young queen who has the broad view that her high
station gives her. As the poem progresses, Levertov shifts more
and more of her formulaic beginnings to the interior sections of
the poem. In the last ten lines, the viewer steps back and surveys
the whole scene. This arrangement echoes those Mother Goose
rhymes which start small and open up like a telescope because of
the accumulated details and their word-for-word repetition. "The
House that Jack Built" is probably the best known example, but a
lesser-known rhyme, "This Is the Key of the Kingdom," is closer
to the spirit of Levertov's poem.

> This is the key of the kingdom:
> In that kingdom is a city.
> In that city is a town,
> In that town there is a street,
> In that street there winds a lane,
> In that lane there is a yard,
> In that yard there is a house,
> In that house there waits a room,
> In that room there is a bed,
> On that bed there is a basket,
>   A basket of flowers.

Flowers in the basket,
Basket on the bed,
Bed in the chamber,
Chamber in the house,
House in the weedy yard,
Yard in the winding lane,
Lane in the broad street,
Street in the high town,
Town in the city,
City in the kingdom:
This is the key of the kingdom.[10]

Why do so many litanies leave us spellbound? Is it because they leap over our powers of reason and let us hear the voice of our ancestral muse, whom some call prayer, some call play, and some call magic?

NOTES

1. Margaret Wise Brown, *Goodnight Moon* (Harper & Row, 1975), u.p.

2. *The Holy Bible,* rev. standard ed. (New York: Thomas Nelson and Sons, 1952), p. 661.

3. Walt Whitman, "Song of Myself," Harold W. Blodgett and Sculley Bradley, eds. (New York: New York University Press, 1965), p. 41.

4. Linda Pastan, "Because," *Carnival Evening* (New York: Norton 1998), p. 107.

5. Christopher Smart, *Jubilate Agno,* W. H. Bond, ed. (London: R. Hart-Davis, 1954), pp. 115–16.

6. Mark Strand, "From a Litany," *Darker* (New York: Atheneum, 1970), p. 26.

7. "The Killer," *Technicians of the Sacred,* Jerome Rothenberg, ed. (Garden City, New York: Anchor, 1969), p. 70.

8. Walt Whitman, "Starting from Paumanok," *Leaves of Grass,* Harold W. Blodgett and Sculley Brandley, eds. (New York: New York University Press, 1965), p. 27.

9. Denise Levertov, "Psalm Concerning the Castle," *The Sorrow Dance* (New York: New Directions, 1966), p. 217.

10. "This is the key of the kingdom," *The Oxford Nursery Rhyme Book,* Iona and Peter Opie, eds. (Oxford: Oxford University Press, 1967), p. 125.

The Left-Handed Story

⤞❦⤝

I MIGHT AS WELL CONFESS right now that when I heard the subject of this panel, "The State of Children's Books in this Millennium and the Next," I felt as if I'd been asked to build a small galaxy, star by star. So I hope you will forgive me if I come here as a writer who looks at the subject through the wrong end of the telescope, a view that lets you believe that even the largest planets can be made to fit in the palm of your hand.

Most of my ideas about what makes a good book for children start with the books I loved as a child. When I grew up and put away childish things, among the things I did not put away were four books: *Through the Looking Glass, The Wizard of Oz, The Snow Queen,* and *The Princess and the Goblin.* It happens that the main characters in these books are girls, but their gender did not attract me so much as their grace under pressure. No matter how dangerous the journey or how curious the companionship, the heroines, possessing no magical powers themselves, hold their own against goblins, witches, and unpleasant queens. But if a wise woman or a talking crow offers advice, they know enough to listen. My favorite passage in *The Snow Queen* is the scene in which Gerda goes to the house of the Finn Woman to ask directions to the Snow Queen's palace, and the reindeer who has accompanied her asks for a potion to make Gerda into a superwoman:

> "You are so clever," said the reindeer finally. "I know you can tie all the winds of the world into four knots on a single thread.

. . . Won't you give this little girl a magic drink so that she gains the strength of twelve men and can conquer the Snow Queen?"

. . . .

"I can't give her any more power than she already has! Don't you understand how great it is? Don't you see how men and animals must serve her; how else could she have come so far, walking on her bare feet!"[1]

It would be hard to say what I learned from these books, for their lessons changed as I changed, and when I read them, I did not imagine that they were teaching me anything. And what books from my childhood did I forget? All the books in which the moral of the story was more important than the story itself.

So when I am writing a book for children, I take care never to ask myself what lessons this book might teach. That is the story's business; my job is to listen to the voice of the story and follow it. And to keep me on track, over my workspace is posted a card bearing a few editorial changes: "Whither thou goest I will go, and where thou lodgest, I will lodge. Thy characters shall be my characters and thy plot my plot."

It has always seemed to me that the story is wiser than the writer. Some time ago an editor at Scholastic asked me to retell the tale of *The Sorcerer's Apprentice*. The only version of the story I knew was the Mickey Mouse sequence in *Fantasia*. The editor sent me a translation of Goethe's poem "Der Zauberlehrling." Though the apprentice in that poem is a boy, I found myself haunted by the image of a girl, perched on a lab stool, surrounded by beakers, bottles, and alembics. You might say that my wish to retell the story started from that image. Here's how my version opens:

> Mount Dragon's Eyes? It's very near,
> yet no one travels it for fear
> of beasts that mutter, huff, and blow,
> round the magician Tottibo.
> Beyond his house the earth looks dead.
> "Take heart, you beasts and bugs," he said.

"Let spiders sing and panthers play.
My new apprentice comes today."

Her bike was blue, her hair was red.
The road turned wicked, sharp, and sly.
The footpath ended in a sigh.
Sylvia dismounted, combed her hair,
took a deep breath and climbed the stair.

On a high stool with silver feet,
a ring of dragons round his seat,
a one-eyed cat, a singing cane
that flexed and scratched its ruby toe,
and other beasts without a name,
sat their fierce master Tottibo

with book and bottle high in hand,
and though the glass held only sand
it shrugged and coiled, reeked and roiled,
sparkled and spankled, beeped and boiled.
Sylvia bowed, a little nervous.
"Your new apprentice, at your service."[2]

Long after the book was published, I realized where that image had come from. My father was a professor of chemistry at the University of Michigan, and when I was in junior high, I would stop by his laboratory to do my homework while he graded blue-books or answered letters. I remember the beakers and test tubes and pipettes, the specimens on the shelves—quartz crystals and pyrite and hematite and mica. In warm weather, when windows were often left open, a white owl would fly in and make itself at home on top of a high wooden bookcase that reached nearly to the ceiling of my father's office. The owl had been raised from an egg by a graduate student in the forestry building, which was located directly opposite the chemistry lab. On one occasion it left a roomful of students speechless when it burst like an emblem of wisdom into a lecture on inorganic chemistry and alighted on the professor's notes. So I saw the sorcerer's apprentice as a girl perched on a lab stool, surrounded by the apparatus of magic. The sorcerer introduces her to a houseful of strange animals, and she is asked to make new clothes for all of them. No easy task. It takes a spectacular failure to remind her that magic is never a shortcut, it is a discipline, and the story ends where it began, but with a difference:

> Mount Dragon's Eyes? It's very near,
> and every day not far from here,
> round a high stool with silver feet,
> those who would study magic meet
> at Tottibo's: the one-eyed cat,
> the drumming panther, singing cane,
> the mice, a dozen dreamy spiders,
> and half a dozen water striders
> that love to conjure up the rain.
> The gryphons dance, the dragons doze;
> they all admired each other 's clothes
> while Sylvia teaches them to say
> the spell she worked out yesterday
> for turning pencils into pails
> and failures into fairy tales.[3]

But perhaps there was a deeper reason why I wanted the apprentice to be a girl. Ten years before I was born my mother had given birth to a boy, who had lived only two days. After my sister was born, my parents hoped their third child would be another boy, to replace the son they had lost. My mother confessed that when I was put into her arms, bald and swaddled and certainly not beautiful, she asked the nurse three times: "Are you sure it isn't a boy?" In a fairy tale, where the third wish often has serious consequences, who knows what might have happened to me? But this was not a fairy tale. While I was growing up, my mother liked to calculate how old her son would be on his birthday. Was he growing up somewhere, she wondered, invisible to us but not to God? And if one day she met her firstborn in heaven, would he recognize her? For of course she could never recognize him.

By the time I'd barely squeaked through high school chemistry with a passing grade, my father knew I would never follow in his footsteps. So in my version of *The Sorcerer's Apprentice* the girl, after some disastrous spells, does what I couldn't do. She has a lab and she makes things happen. If she is not a chemist, she is at least an alchemist.

Now, none of this was in my mind when I wrote the story. But a left-handed story has a subtext that the author is scarcely aware of, yet it shapes the surface narrative the way dreams make out of the stuff of our waking life stories that seem to have been composed by a stranger. And I think many of the children's books that stayed with me are left-handed stories. That is, they are stories written not just from what you know but from more than you know.

I have occasionally received letters from readers whose interpretations of something I've written are so completely different from what I intended that we hardly seem to be talking about the same book. Several years ago I wrote a book called *The High Glorious Skittle Skat Roarious Sky Pie Angel Food Cake.*

It's about a girl who sneaks down to the kitchen at midnight to bake her mother a surprise birthday cake and meets three angels, who have come to sample the cake. She looks up and sees the angels peering into the oven:

> "It's been a long time since we've tasted a cake made at the hands of a mortal child," said the biggest angel.
>
> "A long time," said the middle one. "In heaven, the Welcome Cakes are made by angels. But I believe yours smells even sweeter."
>
> I could hardly believe my ears.
>
> "You smelled my cake in heaven?"
>
> The angels nodded.
>
> "Irresistible," said the smallest angel.
>
> "Divine," added the middle angel.
>
> "In heaven, when people arrive after a long journey," said the biggest angel, "they're invited to sit at the heavenly table."[4]

The conversation continues to the final stages of the baking, cooling, and eating—with the girl concerned about presenting her mother with a less-than-complete cake.

After the book was published, I received a letter from Maryallyn Dennison, used here with her permission:

> Thank you for *The High Rise Glorious Skittle Skat Roarious Sky Pie Angel Food Cake*. Your story made a huge difference for me, my husband, and my daughters, Emmalee and Hannah. I found this book by chance at the Library and brought it home to read to the girls because Hannah loves to cook. . . . Shortly after we first read the story, we learned that Hannah's cancer had returned, and she had only a short time to live. Her first response to the prospect of death was, "It'll be just like that book!"
>
> We read it a few more times over the past weeks. Hannah often spoke excitedly about not only eating, but also baking Welcome Cakes. Two days ago she died in her sleep. It's been a comfort to us to envision her busy with Welcome Cakes. Thank you so much for this gift, which eased Hannah's transition from life to death for all of us.

Now death was the farthest thing from my mind when I wrote the book. But if you believe that the story knows more than the writer, you know that "out of sight" does not mean "out of mind," and if there are angels in the kitchen, you might say that death is already present, a silent witness who watches from the wings. The truth is, you have no idea how your book may take root in your reader's mind. And this is as true for picture books as it is for illustrated stories.

Cake, owl, snow—for me the fairy tales have always affirmed the uncommon life of common things. Isn't this one of the reasons we cherish the books we loved as children, books that showed us a way to let go of our childhood without losing the part of ourselves that still wants to look through the wrong end of the telescope and knows that even the largest planet can be made to fit in the palm of your hand?

NOTES

1. Hans Christian Andersen, "The Snow Queen," *The Complete Fairy Tales and Stories,* Erik Christian Haugaard, trans. (New York: Doubleday, 1974), p. 257.

2. Maryallyn Dennison, Letter to Nancy Willard, October 10, 1995.

3. Nancy Willard, *The Sorcerer's Apprentice* (New York: Blue Sky Press, 1993), n.p.

4. Nancy Willard, *The High Rise Glorious Skittle Skat Roarious Sky Pie Angel Food Cake* (San Diego, California: Harcourt Brace, 1990) n.p.

A Tale out of Time

I RECENTLY ASKED MY STUDENTS in a class on the history of fairy tales a simple question: What was your favorite fairy tale when you were growing up, and how did you find it? Or, to put it differently, how did that particular tale find you? These are students who grew up with computers and who are so adept at finding their way around the World Wide Web that it seems no secrets are hidden from them; there are no doors that can't be opened when you know the password or the command. If Rumplestiltskin appeared to them and said, "Guess my name," they would know a hundred ways of finding it. They are perfectly comfortable in rooms that do not exist in the physical world, meeting and conversing with people whose cloak of invisibility makes them as fictive and dangerous as anyone they might meet in a fairy tale. A *world wide web*—the very name strikes my ear as the invention of a spider of great power, and woe betide the traveler who gets caught in it.

It's no surprise that many of my students came to fairy tales through Disney's reshaping of them. It's also no surprise that the students who remembered hearing the original stories had parents who knew the importance of reading aloud to their children. But however they came to the stories, they discovered that what they remembered of each tale and what they had carried for years like a talisman was not the plot but a scene, a character, or an image buried deep in the shadow of the main event. I have come to believe that none of the transformations that happen in fairy tales—beast into prince, pumpkin into coach—are as astonishing as those that happen to the stories in the minds of those who reread and reinvent them. What you forgot tells you something about who you were when you first heard or read the tale. What you remember tells you something about the magic of the tales themselves, in which one's destiny dwells in ordinary objects: a slipper, a comb, a lamp, waiting to be recognized. Revisiting a fairy tale is like revisiting a house you knew as a child, only to discover there are rooms you never explored and floors you did not even know existed. For me that house is my grandmother's house in Owosso, Michigan, which was torn down long ago to make room for the new post office. Before I can consider the house as a metaphor for remembering fairy tales, I have to tell you a little about that particular house.

If I tell you it was a large white house with many rooms, and that there hung in the vestibule a chandelier on which gleamed dozens of cut-glass tears, do not imagine for a moment that my grandmother's house was a castle, or even a mansion. For years and years the cut-glass tears had been falling, gradually, leaving bare patches on the tarnished brass fixture. My grandmother rented all the upstairs rooms and one of the downstairs rooms as well, and she did all the cleaning of those rooms for the tenants. She made the beds, she dusted the bureaus and windowsills, she scrubbed the floors, the fixtures, and the walls. Whenever she found a glass tear she would tuck it into a kitchen drawer that was already crammed with handles, screws, brackets, old nails, and unidentifiable parts of defunct appliances.

The family lived on the first floor, in the humblest and darkest rooms. My grandfather was an osteopath who kept in his office a cuckoo clock that no longer kept time and held a bird that no longer sang. But what did it matter? My grandparents took the measure of time not by clocks but by the look of the light. "Let's walk to the drugstore while it's still light," or "Time to start dinner. It'll be dark soon." The office was connected by a hallway to a storeroom crammed with tables and chairs wrapped in brown paper, bought at discount and never used. Beyond the bedroom lay a kitchen with a tiny bathroom stuck on like an afterthought.

The hallway had been converted into my grandfather's treatment room, which held a padded table that looked about as comfortable as an ironing board. Behind the glass doors of a small cabinet, phials of medicine stood like potions.

When my mother and sister and I visited, we slept in whatever room happened to be available. If all the rooms were rented, I slept in the kitchen on a cot. There was but one downstairs tenant, an elderly widow named Mrs. Harris, whom we never saw but whose existence we could never forget. One morning, my mother could not find her shoes; having searched for an hour, she was ready to give up, but just then Mrs. Harris called out like Thisbe to Pyramus from the other side of the wall: "Did you look behind the radiator?"

In that same town there was a castle, a very small castle, built on the banks of the Shiawassee River by a writer named James Oliver Curwood, who for years had longed to live in a castle and whose popular novels had earned enough so that he got his wish, accomplished not by magic but by cold, hard cash. Having seen no other castles, I thought Curwood's castle, with its arched doors and diamond windowpanes, the most enchanted residence imaginable. Years later I returned to Owosso for a visit, and since the castle was now open to the public, I stepped inside. The rooms were few and had been turned into offices. No giants, no ogres, thank goodness. And, alas, no fairy godmothers.

So when I think of a house as the metaphor for remembering fairy tales, when I think of a place full of rooms to be explored and scenes to be enjoyed, I do not think of a castle. No, I think of my grandmother's house, crammed with ordinary inconveniences and alive with the voices of real people who paid rent and went off to work in the morning. What made the place like a fairy tale for me? The hidden lives? The spaces I didn't know upstairs? The memory I had of once (and only once, because I was ill) of being put in a newly vacated upstairs room full of light that illuminated a marble sink, perfectly egg-shaped, a room I never saw again? I would have thought it was a dream if my mother had not said,

"Yes, there was such a room. It was the most expensive room in the house."

We all know that fairy tales are as full of familiar things as your grandmother's pantry or my grandmother's sink, with its stove and its bin of apples and its bit of mirror stuck in the tiny bathroom off the kitchen and its row of boots and slippers by the back door and its *Farmers' Almanac*, with the phases of the moon like a secret alphabet making its way with small steps down the calendar pages. The apples in that kitchen were not golden, the mirror did not speak, the slippers were not glass, the boots could not carry you seven leagues, and the useful advice in the almanac would never transform your life, though it might keep the moles out of your garden or prevent the clothespins from freezing to the line. And because neither our lives by day nor our dreams by night are really ordinary at all, and because things hidden wait for someone to find them (whether it be a shoe behind the radiator or a scrap of memory), when you go back to the fairy tales you find that you experience them differently; you find that cannot step into the same tale twice. The tale has not changed, but the reader, no longer a child, enters by a different door. So when my students return to their favorite fairy tales, they find that what they need from the stories has always been there, waiting for them to recognize it.

As a teacher, I try to open those doors for my students. As a poet, I go back to the fairy tales, looking for what first called me to them: the miracle of time itself, into which we are born and from which we will depart. I go back to the three tales that showed me the experience of time without hours, minutes, and seconds: "Mother Holle" from the Brothers Grimm; "Vasilisa the Beautiful," a Russian tale; and "The Seven Doves," an Italian tale that may not be as familiar to many readers as the other two.

"Mother Holle" is a story I have carried with me on the long journey from innocence to experience, like a living candle in the heart. Everyone will recognize the character of the abused stepdaughter who is forced to sit by a well and spin, until the day she accidentally drops the reel of her spindle into the water. In desperation, she leaps in after it, loses consciousness, and wakes to find herself in a sunlit meadow full of flowers. Here the girl is hired by an old woman to keep house. The girl's first impression of her employer is not a good one. The text says, "She had such big teeth that the maiden was scared and wanted to run away."

In spite of her big teeth, I was disposed to like Mother Holle, for she seemed a close relative of all those mysterious old women in Mother Goose. She is close kin to the woman who lives under the hill ("and if she's not gone, she lives there still"). And she is at least a first cousin to the woman who ascends in a basket with her broom in her hand, not riding on it to some Witch's Sabbath but putting the broom to the use for which it was intended:

> There was an old woman tossed up in a basket,
> Seventeen times as high as the moon;
> Where she was going, I couldn't but ask it,
> For in her hand she carried a broom.
> Old woman, old woman, old woman, quoth I,
> Where are you going to up so high?
> To brush the cobwebs off the sky!
> May I go with you? Aye, by-and-by.[1]

Too much Sunday school had made me a little nervous about following strangers into the heavens, lest I wouldn't be allowed to return. But Mother Holle invites no such fears. The story tells us that "the old woman cried after her, 'Why are you afraid, my dear child? Stay with me, and if you do all the housework properly, everything will turn out well for you. Only you must make my bed nicely and carefully and give it a good shaking so the feathers fly. Then it will snow on earth, for I am Mother Holle.'"[2]

What's in a name? Her name, of course, means Hell, which in Old English, spelled with one *l*, names the queen of the dead in Scandinavian mythology, whose home was reserved for the spirits of ordinary citizens who died in their beds, not in battle, and were therefore not bound for Valhalla.

The story does not tell us very much about what to me is the most fascinating part of the tale, the girl's life with this goddess of the dead turned domestic weather lady. We are told she spent "a long time" with Mother Holle, who was pleased with the girl's work, yet a season passes before our eyes in a single sentence. "In return, the woman treated her well, and she gave her roasted or boiled meat every day." What kind of meat did they eat and where did it come from? And what did Mother Holle's house look like? The girl would have known it intimately, for nothing acquaints you with a house more quickly than cleaning it. When, I wonder, did the girl notice the absence of bells to mark the passing of human time—wedding bells, church bells, death knells? What did the young girl and the old woman talk about? In the evening, did they tell stories? Did Mother Holle tell her a story she'd heard long ago, perhaps from another visitor, a story about the Month Brothers, the twelve men who sit on twelve chairs on a rocky plateau on a distant woods, and pass the staff of time from one brother to the next? Did the girl say, "Oh, I know that story. When January holds the staff, there is snow. When June holds the staff, there are strawberries. When September holds the staff there are apples"? Did Mother Holle chuckle at their names and remind the girl that those who change the seasons are far older than the Gregorian calendar?

What looks like a death by drowning—the girl's arrival into the underground world through the water in the well—turns out to be a rebirth, a kind of baptism by total immersion. And what calls me back to the story is the journey back home and the girl's reason for making it. "I've got a tremendous longing to return home, and even though everything is wonderful down here, I've got to return to my people."[3] Pleased with her request, Mother Holle leads her to a large door, which has not been mentioned before, and opens it. Gold showers down on the girl as a reward for her industry. More marvelous than the opening of the door is the closing of it, after which we are told that "the maiden found herself back up on earth, not far from her mother's house." In her end is her beginning, and surely she has been as changed by her departure from the things of this world as if she had indeed returned from the dead. Now she is back in the world, and the circle of her journey is complete. What did the girl learn about the world during her retreat from it and about herself from her sojourn with Mother Holle? And what did Mother Holle learn about homesickness and the condition of being human?

The wise women of the fairy tales have many relatives, and some of them would rather devour their guests than feed them. How fortunate for the girl that she found Mother Holle and not Baba Yaga, the old woman who rides through the Russian forests in a mortar and pestle and whose hut turns and turns on its unlikely foundation, a pair of chicken legs. Her fence is made of human bones, spiked with human skulls. The posts of her door are human legs, the bolts that close it are human hands, the lock is a mouth full of sharp teeth.

The beautiful Vasilisa is sent by her stepsisters to fetch light from Baba Yaga, so they can finish their tasks. There are easier ways to fetch light; their underlying motive is to get rid of their competition. Vasilisa's two-day journey is measured not in miles or hours but in the coming of light and dark: daybreak, sunrise, and nightfall pass the girl on the road to the witch's house.

> Suddenly a horseman galloped past her: his face was white, he was dressed in white, his horse was white, and his horse's trappings were white—daybreak came to the woods.
>
> She walked on farther, and a second horseman galloped past her: he was all red, he was dressed in red, and his horse was red—the sun began to rise.
>
> Vasilisa walked the whole night and the whole day, and only on the following evening did she come to the glade where Baba Yaga's hut stood. . . . Suddenly another horseman rode by. He was all black, he was dressed in black, and his horse was black. He galloped up to Baba Yaga's door and vanished, as through the earth had swallowed him up—night came.[4]

Time's messengers are surely more dangerous than the bones of the dead: the dead might feel a twinge of sympathy for the girl, but time carries out its duties without mercy. If an uninvited guest of great power decrees that your daughter shall prick her finger on a spinning wheel and die, even a wise godmother can't undo all the damage and you must settle for a modified curse of a hundred years' sleep.

Much is shown and nothing is explained in Baba Yaga's house, including the identity of the souls who once inhabited the skulls and her relationship with the three horsemen. Baba Yaga tells Vasilisa that "all of them are my faithful servants." What is her power and how far does it reach? Is it so great that she can command the sun to rise? That she is in league with time is certain. Her house is made of time. When darkness falls, the eyes of the skulls on her fence gleam until "the glade was as bright as day." When morning breaks, the eyes of the skulls fade and go out. You might say that Baba Yaga had the first automatic timer and she powered it herself.

With her sharp teeth and her command of natural events, she is the fierce sister of Mother Holle. Was Baba Yaga once a guardian of the hearth, to whom was assigned the broom, the pestle, and the mortar? Was she a guardian of both the living and the dead, giving life and taking the living back into the earth from which they came?

The fairy tales give a face and a name to what in real life is everywhere and nowhere: the mystery of time when it is not measured by clocks or when it is not measured at all, the way time had abandoned the cuckoo clock in my grandmother's house. Instead of telling time, it told us its story, which was carved all around the face of the clock: two cuckoos alighting on the edge of a nest feed their hatchlings.

Fairy tales that showed the secret life of time when it was off-duty were a great comfort to me, because when it came to telling time, I was a very slow learner. My mother, always an optimist, bought me a picture book with a toy clock in it, and the clock had movable hands. Though I could easily read the o'clocks—seven o'clock, eight o'clock, and so forth—I couldn't get the hang of what happened in the spaces between them. It was perfectly clear that time passed at different speeds, quickly if you were happy, slowly if you were bored. Grown-ups spoke of losing an hour or not knowing where the time went. Nothing on the face of the clock in my book or the clock in our kitchen took this into consideration. So whenever my mother asked me, "What time is it?" I would answer truthfully, "The big hand is at three and the little hand is at four," unless the hands stood on the hour, which was something you could give a name to: four o'clock, or noon.

To complicate matters, the picture on our calendar for January showed Father Time, an elderly man in a toga holding a scythe, much like the one in use on my great-grandfather's farm. I knew what the scythe cut down did not rise again. Its purpose was to clear space for the next sowing, the next generation. Perhaps that is why time, when he appears as a character in fairy tales, is sometimes accompanied by a wise crone who remembers how, in her day, time passed in weather and light and seasons that came round again and again.

But does time itself have a local habitation? For the teller of fairy tales, nothing is impossible. "The Seven Doves" contains the most vivid account I know of time's living arrangements—or perhaps we should say his dying arrangements. In Time's house, artlessly furnished with broken statues and shattered columns, the walls are cracking, the foundations crumbling, the doors wormeaten. Files, saws, scythes, sickles, and pruning hooks litter the ground, along with Time's trophies: thousands of small earthen jars that bear the names of cities Time has conquered. Only his coat-of-arms over the door has escaped destruction. Quartered, it shows a stag, a raven, a phoenix, and a serpent biting its tail.

But the story can't begin until Channa, a young woman whose seven brothers have been turned into doves by an ogre, learns that only the Mother of Time can tell her how to break the spell. On her quest to find Time's house, she meets an old pilgrim who tells her what to expect and how to behave. She is to hide herself until Time flies out, leaving his mother in charge, seated upon a large clock that is fastened to the wall.

As soon as you enter, quickly take the weights off the clock. Then call the old woman, and beg her to answer your questions; whereupon she will instantly command her son to eat you up. But the clock having lost its weights, her son cannot move, and she will therefore be obliged to tell you what you wish. But do not trust any oath she may make, unless she swears by the wings of her son. If she does so, trust her; do what she tells you, and you will be content.[5]

All happens as the pilgrim has predicted, and when Channa lets go of the weights, she kisses the old woman's hand, "which had a mouldy smell." Touched by this gesture, the old woman tells her to hide behind the door and promises to find out all she wishes to know. "And as soon as he goes out again—for he never stays quiet in one place—you can depart. But do not let yourself be heard or seen, for he is such a glutton that he does not spare even his own children, and when all fails, he devours himself, and then springs up anew."

The original tale, which must have been a variant of the more familiar "The Six Swans" from the Brothers Grimm, has been embellished by a literary hand. The animals on Time's coat-of-arms were assigned by an imagination that loved allegories, and their symbolic presence reinforces the message: stop the clock and you can stop the only time that matters in this tale, the time allotted for a human life. No falling down wells or shaking the snow out of featherbeds here, and no messengers waking the sun or bringing the darkness home to roost. The junkyard of Time is crammed with the tools of human lives and the dust of human triumphs. It reminds me of the storeroom in my grandmother's house. Even Time is bound by the human contrivance of a clock, and he must enter his house by a door, behind which a human visitor may safely hide. Wherever a door opens, a threshold appears, and a threshold signals a new beginning.

What do I want my students, many of whom are fledgling writers reading some of these tales for the first time, to take with them into their own lives and writing?

May they never forget that a fairy tale is like a house that can be entered by many doors, and behind every door lies a new story. Take, for example, the Grimm tale "The Worn-Out Dancing Shoes" (called "The Twelve Dancing Princesses" in Andrew Lang's version) about the twelve princesses who escape every night, through a trapdoor in their bedroom, to a glittering underground estate where they dance all night with twelve princes, of whom we know nothing except an odd fact that the storyteller reveals in the last sentence: "The princes, however, were compelled to remain under a curse for as many nights as they had danced with the princesses." Who put this curse on them, and for what reason, we are never told. However, one of my students decided to find out. He wrote an elegant story in which one of the princes describes his life before his stepmother banished him and his eleven brothers to the underground kingdom. As he said in his preface, "I am writing this story to explore the unwritten element of the story, and to find out what happens in the spaces between the words."[6]

Fairy tales are as luminous and layered as an onion. When I tell my students that a fairy tale is like a house they can enter by many doors, I also tell them they can find those doors even if they've forgotten the story. There is a difference between forgetting a story and forgetting about a story. The story you forget about vanishes, the story you forget will return when you need it. When you forget a story, it does not forget you. Like the houses we live in, stories are a shelter and a station; a place to keep us and a place of departure. Though Time takes us all in the end, he gives each of us a beginning and puts us into a story, in which some are tellers and others are listeners who will pass the tales on to other tellers and other listeners.

And what, in the end, do I wish for my students?

May their best stories, born in time, live outside of it. I wish those stories a good journey.

NOTES

1. *The Oxford Nursery Rhyme Book,* Iona and Peter Opie, eds. (London: Clarendon, 1987), p. 70.

2. "Mother Holle," *The Complete Fairy Tales of the Brothers Grimm,* Jack Zipes, trans. (New York: Bantam, 2002), p. 89.

3. Ibid.

4. "Vasilisa the Beautiful," *Russian Fairy Tales,* Norbert Guterman, trans. (New York: Pantheon, 1973), p. 441.

5. "The Seven Doves," *The Italian Fairy Book,* Anne Macdonald, trans. (New York: Frederick A. Stokes, 1911), p. 128.

6. Bradford Louryk, "The Eleventh Dancing Prince: A Memoir." Unpublished.

Crossing the Water

LAST SPRING I strolled into Barnes and Noble with the intention of buying a cup of coffee and noticed a rack of beautifully bound books set up near the entrance. You know the kind of books I'm talking about: those seductive blank journals, full of possibility, that invite you to record your own wishes, lies, and dreams. At first glance it seemed to me that I had stepped into the travel section, for on the covers of the handsomest books glowed beautifully printed maps of the world—the world as it looked to the early cartographers who thought the earth was flat as a dinner plate. At the ocean's borders the early mapmakers had drawn the monsters that awaited unlucky sailors who fell off the earth into the darkness that surrounded it. You know the kind of darkness they had in mind. In the beginning God created heaven and earth, and darkness was upon the face of the deep.

But the covers of the less expensive books showed the brighter side of travel. There were snapshot albums covered with imitation leather and fake stickers from famous hotels. There were postcard albums papered with postcards of the Eiffel Tower, not real postcards, of course, but printed as they might be on fine wrapping paper. There was a journal with a balloon on the cover rising over the words *A Record of My Travels,* which organized your experience into Restaurants, Hotels, and Addresses, leaving very little space for each of them and no space at all for conversations or sights not found in the guidebook.

Behind the travel books I spied another rack of blank books, some of them titled *Journal,* one of them called *Dreams.* They were bound in paper printed with clouds, the sunrise, the night sky. Though the pages were empty, they were not entirely blank. The edifying comments that appeared at the bottom of each page included poems, suggestions for meditation, and encouraging quotations. A quote from Lao-tsu. A quote from a poem by Emily Dickinson, which I'd memorized in high school.[1]

> Because I could not stop for Death—
> He kindly stopped for me—
> The Carriage held but just Ourselves—
> And Immortality.
>
> We slowly drove—He knew no haste
> And I had put away
> My labor and my leisure too,
> For His Civility—
>
> We passed the School, where Children strove
> At Recess—in the Ring—
> We passed the Fields of Gazing Grain—
> We passed the Setting Sun—
>
> Or rather—He passed Us—
> The Dews drew quivering and chill—
> For only Gossamer, my Gown—
> My Tippet—only Tulle—
>
> We paused before a House that seemed
> A Swelling of the Ground—
> The Road was scarcely visible—
> The Cornice—in the Ground—
>
> Since then—'tis Centuries—and yet
> Feels shorter than the Day
> I first surmised the Horses' Heads
> Were toward Eternity—

It appeared I had not left the travel section after all, only stepped back into a different wing of it. The travelers who chose one of these books needed no maps. The journey itself is the destination. It's the kind of journey the painter Joan Miró had in mind when he said, "If you have any notion of where you are going, you will never get anywhere." It's the kind of journey you find in fairy tales. I am especially fond of the Russian tale in which the hero is given the following command: *Go I know not whither and fetch me I know not what.* Getting started is the easy part, because the journey of a thousand miles and a walk around the block both begin with a single step.

With magical and spiritual journeys, what matters most is not where you are going but who you are when you get there.

Let me tell you about the first time I took such a journey. My journey starts in a small town in Michigan, and I did not know it was a spiritual journey when I took it, for it had a very practical purpose: learning to swim. Imagine a gaggle of cottages running in a single line along a dirt road. If you walked down that road on a summer day, you would see on one side of the road a broad field that opened up behind the cottages and at the far end of the field a forest. On the other side you would see a lake, though you could not see all of it at once. The lake was a mile across and a hundred feet deep in the middle. No buildings stood on the far shore, the periphery of which was guarded by a sinister garden of underwater weeds that were especially hospitable to bloodsuckers and crayfish. Long rubbery stems vanished into darkness. If you could swim over the weeds without being caught, you stepped onto a thin clearing slathered with small slippery stones. The far shore was rarely visited by people, but cows grazed in the pasture among a smattering of birch trees. Because the lake was deep and boating accidents were a common occurrence, children growing up near the water were taught to swim at a young age. In our family the test for any child who wanted to prove he or she could swim was simple. Swim across the lake and back without a life jacket. And bring back a bit of the bark from the birch trees to prove you'd really made it to the far shore.

It was my mother who taught me to swim when I was seven years old. The life jacket she buckled me into consisted of a canvas strap, to which were fastened chunks of balsa wood. Each day she took out one chunk of wood, until I was swimming with only the canvas strap holding me up, or so I thought until my mother said to me, "That strap isn't doing a thing for you. You're swimming on your own."

So I made my journey to the far shore. Is that the end of the story? Hardly. As we all know, journeys are teachers, and often they teach us more than we ever set out to learn. Swimming across a vast expanse of dark water, you learn something about strength and something about courage. You cross deep water by taking it one stroke at a time. When you grow tired you lie on your back and float till you are rested. Sometimes the only way you can cross the water is to make a boat of yourself.

Perhaps because I was born on the thumb of a left-handed mitten stretched out over five lakes, I've always imagined that significant journeys include crossing water. The River Styx, the River Jordan, Lethe the River of Forgetfulness—call it what you will. As a child I heard my aunt tell of the journey her soul took when she was so ill that everyone around her had given her up for dead. Below her she saw her body lying on the bed, before her she saw a river, and on the far side of the river stood the relatives who had recently died and the ancestors known to her only through photographs.

"Come over," they called.

My aunt's soul thought about it. She was only fifteen years old and not ready to leave this life just yet, thank you, so she glided back into her body, got well, and lived another seventy years. Sometimes you want to cross the water, sometimes you want to find the way home. Finding the way home is not always easy, especially if you are driving down Route 55 and find yourself so engrossed in conversation that you miss your exit. If you are not in a hurry, getting lost has its good side. When I was a child bicycling around our neighborhood, I would try to lose my way on purpose so I could have that grateful shock of recognition when I rediscovered the familiar streets that led to my house, that place inhabited by the people I loved, that place where I was known and loved in spite of all my failings. My favorite moment in *The Wizard of Oz*—and I'm speaking of the book here, not the movie—is the last chapter, which is less than half a page:

> Aunt Em had just come out of the house to water the cabbages when she looked up and saw Dorothy running toward her.
>
> "My darling child!" she cried, folding the little girl in her arms and covering her face with kisses; "where in the world did you come from?"
>
> "From the Land of Oz," said Dorothy, gravely. "And here is Toto, too. And oh, Aunt Em! I'm so glad to be at home again!"[2]

If there is a moral here, it's a simple one. If you never get lost, you may never be found.

Many writers have described the overwhelming feeling of losing one's sense of direction in a poem or story that comes just before a breakthrough, an insight that shows you exactly how to finish it. My father was a chemist who worked at chemistry problems in much the same way I work at a poem. He would sit at the dining room table with his papers in front of him, and he would work at a problem until he got stuck and could go no further. Then he would rise from the table and say, "I give up." But I knew this was only a ritual that allowed the magic to happen. A man who has given up does not go to bed with a pen and a notebook on his bedside table. What he really meant was "I'm letting go." I'm letting go, so that something else—call it intuition, call it inspiration, call it faith in the limits of human reason—can take your confusion and show you the order that was there all along, waiting for you to find it.

I am sure that many of you are familiar with the spiritual exercise of walking the labyrinth. What is a labyrinth but the opposite of a shortcut? It is a road designed to slow you down on your journey. It is a way of losing yourself, of giving the words of Jesus a new context: He that findeth his life shall lose it, and he that loseth his life . . . shall find it. The labyrinth need not be vast. The labyrinth engraved on a portion of the floor in a cathedral—

Chartres, for example—will do just as well if you want to step out of the world's way to examine your life.

Let me tell about a second journey I made across water. Many summers ago my husband Eric and I came as teachers to Star Island off the coast of New Hampshire. Eric taught a workshop in photography, and I taught one in writing for children. My memories from that place return as a series of images, now freed from the time frame in which they occurred.

The winding path to the chapel, the light of the candles that showed us the path and each other.

The sea that bound us to this place and that had nothing to do with human notions of geography.

The gulls fiercely guarding their nests on the bare rocks.

The camera obscura built by one of Eric's students: a small dark room on the back wall of which was projected the image—upside down—of islanders making their way over the rocks. It was a little like standing in Plato's cave and seeing both the shadows and the world that made them. When you return to the mainland, you are not quite the same person who left it, and that is the reason for labyrinths, pilgrimages, and island retreats. The journey itself is the destination.

Our memories, too, make journeys. What is lost comes back to find us when we need to be found. Not until after my mother's death did I understand what my mother's swimming lessons had really taught me.

SWIMMING LESSONS

A mile across the lake, the horizon bare
or nearly so: a broken sentence of birches.
No sand. No voices calling me back.
Waves small and polite as your newly washed hair
push the slime-furred pebbles like pawns,
an inch here. Or there.

You threaded five balsa blocks on a strap
and buckled them to my waist, a crazy life
vest for your lazy little daughter.

Under me, green deepened to black.
You said, "Swim out to the deep water."
I was seven years old. I paddled forth

and the water held me. Sunday you took away
one block, the front one. I stared down
at my legs, so small, so nervous and pale,
not fit for a place without roads.
Nothing in these depths had legs or need of them
except the toeless foot of the snail.

Tuesday you took away two more blocks.
Now I could somersault and stretch.
I could scratch myself against trees like a cat.
I even made peace with the weeds that fetch
swimmers in the noose of their stems
while the cold lake puckers and preens.

Friday the fourth block broke free. "Let it go,"
you said. When I asked you to take
out the block that kept jabbing my heart,
I felt strong. This was the sixth day.
For a week I wore the only part
of the vest that bothered to stay:

a canvas strap with nothing to carry.
The day I swam away from our safe shore,
you followed from far off, your stealthy oar
raised, ready to ferry me home
if the lake tried to keep me.
Now I watch the tides of your body

pull back from the hospital sheets.
"Let it go," you said. "Let it go." My heart is not afraid of deep
    water.
It is wearing its life vest,
that invisible garment of love
and trust, and it tells you this story.[3]

NOTES

1. *The Complete Poems of Emily Dickinson,* Thomas H. Johnson, ed. (Boston: Little, Brown, 1960), p. 350.

2. L. Frank Baum, "Chapter XXIV: Home Again," *The Wonderful Wizard of Oz* (New York: Dover, 1960), 261.

3. Nancy Willard, "Swimming Lessons," *Swimming Lessons: New and Selected Poems* (New York: Knopf, 1996), pp. 3–4.

Portraits and Interviews

The Sorcerer's Apprentice:
A Conversation with Harry Roseman,
Assistant to Joseph Cornell

⟨∞⟩

WILLARD: Harry, tell me how you found the job working as Joseph Cornell's assistant.

ROSEMAN: In the summer of 1969, I came down to New York, because Cathy [the painter Catherine Murphy] had enrolled in Queens College for graduate school. We were living in Massachusetts and getting ready to relocate to New York. In the late summer I came down to the city from Massachusetts to look for an apartment and do an errand for Cathy at Queens College. So I went to the office, and I was trying to get this little bit of bureaucratic paperwork done. Helen Schiavo, the acting chairman, was the only person who could solve the problem and she wasn't there. So someone in the office got her on the phone at home, and we got into this conversation. So first we did the business part, and we really liked each other. We had this long conversation. How do I say this? Not being overly shy myself, at a certain point I felt comfortable enough to also ask her if she knew of any jobs. She told me she knew Joseph Cornell, and she thought he was looking for an assistant, and she could set up an interview. I was just thrilled. It was a couple of years after that terrific Guggenheim show, which I saw. So I said absolutely, sure. She said she'd set up an interview and get back to me and work it all out. So that's how the interview happened.

She had organized a show of his at Queens College sometime before. She told me a little about his mother and about his brother. She also said he'd probably know right away if he was going to hire me the minute I came in. And then she told me one secret. She said, however the interview went, I shouldn't leave without an answer. This was the key: if I leave and he says he's going to let me know, he's going to have to think about it, I'd probably never hear from him again. So the key was, not to leave without a definitive answer.

She also told me about his reticence and his slowness to let you in, in any way whatsoever.

WILLARD: What was the interview like?

ROSEMAN: After the interview was set up, I went out to see him. First we sat in the yard. I knocked on the front door, and he said, "Come round." He brought me round and we sat in the yard and talked for a little while. But there were a lot of planes flying overhead, so it was a bit hard to hear.

Then he said, "We'll go to the porch." He told me to walk around to the front of the house, and he went through the house and let me in, almost like starting again. And we sat on the porch, and he took notes while we were talking. We talked for a while and then we went into the house. He said, "Okay, let's go inside and I'll show you around." I thought that was a big step. Then he showed me around the house and he even took me down to the studio. The interview went on for quite a while. At a certain point he said he'd let me know. That was my cue to say, Well, I need to know right now. What I said was, "I have plans to make and I really do need to know, now." Which is something I would never have thought of saying. He said, "Okay, we'll give it a try, but don't think you're working in my studio on my work. We're not doing that." I think that was a way for him to make sure I didn't want something from him he wasn't willing to give. And I didn't at the time think that that something was literally working on the work. He wanted me to care about his work, but he didn't want me to come as some sort of fan, because even later on he talked about people who kept calling him to come and work for nothing.

And he didn't like that idea so much. Even though I think he probably didn't pay all his assistants, he still wanted it to be professional. Maybe it was also a way of testing me, to see if I only had one thing in mind about this job: to get into his head, into his psyche through his work. And he said what I'd be doing mostly was correspondence, cataloguing. I said fine.

WILLARD: How long did you work for him?

ROSEMAN: I started in September 1969, and I worked for him until 1972. He died late in 1972. By the time he died, I was very fond of him. My guess is, all his relationships were complicated.

WILLARD: Do you remember your impressions of the house? I don't mean just what it looked like but your first impression of what it felt like being there.

ROSEMAN: I have a very clear idea about the house. I could probably describe every stick of furniture in it. But my sense of the house is a combination of first impressions and being there over a three-year period.

WILLARD: When you visualize the house at this moment, what specifically do you remember?

ROSEMAN: I remember the darkness. It felt dark. Not that it always was. It just felt dark and it felt different than what was outside. There was this darkness and this quality of air, and there was something about spending the whole day in that house that made you feel you were in another time zone.

WILLARD: Was it crowded with things?

ROSEMAN: Yes, it was crowded. I think of it as organized chaos. It looked kind of messy. I mean, there were piles of books and letters and papers, and plenty of furniture, which I assume was the same furniture that was there when he lived with his mother and his brother. So it was like a very cozy lower-middle-class house but overlaid with clues of something else, with piles of stuff and little special objects and collages leaning against walls and in boxes and a certain amount of messiness. It wasn't neat anymore; it wasn't like most people's mothers would want their house.

WILLARD: Do you remember the kinds of objects that struck you, over time?

ROSEMAN: Over time? Well, the whole thing was such a piece to me. Him, the house, the studio, time, it all kind of hung together. Some days I would look at one thing and some days I would look at another thing. But it didn't separate. I worked a lot for him.

WILLARD: Did you have a schedule?

ROSEMAN: Sometimes I worked four days a week. Sometimes three days a week. Sometimes ten till three, sometimes nine till four. Sometimes afternoon through evening.

WILLARD: He'd call so you'd know the hours?

ROSEMAN: We'd sort of talk about them ahead of time.

WILLARD: What kind of work did he ask you to do?

ROSEMAN: Strangely enough, when I started early in September, all we did for weeks was to work on his work. We went right down to the studio, and at one point I made some sort of reference to the fact that I had thought I'd be doing something else, and he looked at me like I'd made the whole thing up. So we just started in the studio right away. Sometimes he'd have me building boxes or putting background paper on boxes, and then sometimes he'd just come down the stairs and sit four stairs from the bottom and watch me for awhile. We started new boxes, and there were many old boxes around in different states. Out of the blue he'd turn around and say, "Bring that box from the shelf," which had clearly been sitting there for years. And we'd go into it and then finish it.

Time was fluid, very fluid.

And others never got finished. But it was like he had put it down just yesterday. He worked in all these very tight series. My feeling about it is, it was a way for him to keep working on these series and not have them die to him, a way for him to be fresh about it and find a new way to go into it.

Eventually he'd send me down to the studio by myself.

WILLARD: In the studio, what work would you do?

ROSEMAN: At first I kind of stood there while he worked and handed him things. "Oh, could you get me that?"

WILLARD: Like a surgical nurse.

ROSEMAN: Yes, like a nurse. And then little by little he had me cut things out, paste things up. Sometimes I would mix these aniline dyes for him, especially this very intense blue that he used a lot. The blue dye came in this fine powder, and we had to mix it up with alcohol to dilute it. It was so potent and so thin that my tongue would be blue, and when I blew my nose it would be blue just from mixing it up, not even putting my face over it. Sometimes it would last for a couple of days. It spooked me. I had a feeling this was not good for me.

Early on, somewhere during those first couple of months, he told me about some assistant who he was furious at and never forgave because she broke one of the wine glasses he was using in a box. He got really angry even talking about it.

One day I was down in the basement by myself. I was working down there, and there was a can of aniline dye on the floor, and I kicked it. There was this worktable that had a slatted bottom, and there were three collages sitting on the floor leaning against it. So when I accidentally kicked the can, it splashed against these collages, and this river ran like lava and started soaking up into the bottoms. I ran around and cleaned it up, and my heart was going boom boom boom boom, and of course that story of the idiotic assistant who broke a glass was looming in my mind.

I got my courage up and went upstairs and said, "I think you should come down and see something. I've had an accident." So he comes down, and I'm standing there like a twelve-year-old boy ready to be admonished. And he looks at the collages, and he looks at me, and he looks at the collages. "I like it," he says. That was so thrilling. I was so tense.

WILLARD: What else did you do for him?

ROSEMAN: I did all kinds of things. I mowed the lawn. I replanted all his grass once. I raked leaves in the fall, and I shoveled the walk a little bit, and I made lunch for him.

WILLARD: This has nothing to do with art, but I can't help asking. What did Cornell like to eat?

ROSEMAN: It's kind of a myth now, how much he loved sweets. Even the stuff he ate for lunch was closer to sweets than to food. Once in a while I'd make him an egg, but that was rare. Lots of times I'd make him frozen sweet potatoes, and then put tons of brown sugar in it so it almost turned to soup. And sometimes regular instant mashed potatoes—he'd eat that. I'm a person who tends not to instinctively eat well, but I was amazed.

I don't think he liked eating in front of people. I think he thought it was kind of private, and sometimes when he was eating with me, he'd put his handkerchief up to his mouth when he chewed. He chewed very fast, very fast little chews.

WILLARD: I think there are some cultures in which the act of eating is a considered a very intimate, private act.

ROSEMAN: Well, there's a French bird you eat that way. You eat the whole little bird, and you eat the head, bones and everything, and you have to eat it behind a cover. I forget if you put a bag on your head or something in front of your face, but you eat it in private, while you're in public. I don't know the exact cultural history, but maybe the idea of watching someone put a whole animal into their mouths may be a little appalling.

So it was like that a little bit when he first started eating with me. Sometimes he also felt—one time he sat down with me and said, "I'm not fit to eat with." And I didn't know what he meant by that. Maybe he knew he had an odd style of eating.

WILLARD: Cornell seems such a rarified sensibility—it makes you wonder why he didn't simply evaporate when he stepped out into the world. In all the photographs I've see of him, he looks so pale.

ROSEMAN: Oh, he was very pale. Pale, pale, pale. He was the palest person I've ever seen. He was very gaunt amid very white. He had no color at all, and he dressed in greys and blacks. He felt like someone in a black and white photograph. Sometimes he'd wear a brown sweater. I have some color photographs of him and some black and white ones, but the black and white ones feel more to me the way he felt in life.

I remember a long time ago there was a joke in the *New Yorker* that showed Proust at a luncheonette counter, and the whole thing was drawn in one way and Proust was washed in another way. And it's just how Cornell looked when he was out in the world. Like somehow he was made of something else, or the world was in color and he was in black and white. When we would leave the house and go on errands and we would be in the street, sometimes I would think of what we must have looked like, walking together. He wore this big loose overcoat. One time we went to downtown Flushing, and we had to meet in this place called the Hurdy Gurdy, which was like a junky food place. I went out and did some errands and came back, and when I looked up at him, he looked like an apparition.

WILLLARD: Apparition does seem the right word for him.

ROSEMAN: He was paler than anyone—I mean, it's hard for me to explain how pale he was. There was something about being in his house with him—he felt one with that place in a certain way so it did not feel strange, but when I was out in the world with him, I was struck by the image be must have made. We'd leave the house together and it would be like leaving a compound, leaving the safety of the village for the world.

He always wore his clothes very large. One time he sent me off shopping for him to get a suit. He was very, very thin, and I think he asked me to get him 36 inch pants. He probably had a 24 or 26 inch waist. Not only was he apparitional because of his color, he was also kind of lost in his clothes.

WILLARD: He anticipated present fashion.

ROSEMAN: And when we went out walking in the street, he would change his pace, just all of a sudden. Sometimes we'd be walking slow, and then we'd speed up for no reason and then slow down and then speed up again. It was like being led by a dance partner. And then sometimes I remember we'd walk to the corner to take the bus to downtown Flushing, for shopping and stuff. (I didn't have a car at that point.) Sometimes I'd stand and he'd find a lightpost, and he'd lean on that. Then the bus would come and he wouldn't move and then all of a sudden he'd make a mad dash for it, like he just got there.

WILLARD: What about the times you arrived and he didn't have any work for you?

ROSEMAN: Sometimes there was a lot of vagueness about my duties. He'd send me down to the cellar, and I was supposed to be working or straightening and I'd have to figure out what to do. And other times I'd be sent out to the garage, to the archives. That was just fun, because mostly I'd just look through things. There was great stuff out there, and I would just open boxes and look through old prints and old French magazines. And the leaves would blow in, and he didn't want me to rake them out. There were parts of things that never got completed. Things got moved sometimes to take on another life in another place.

There was one corner of the garage where he used to talk about us making a kind of altar for his mother. There were old family photos up on the walls in the house, and there was a picture of him with his father, both of them as adults, which never happened, because his father died when Cornell was fourteen. It was a montage. And I said, "Was your father a nice man?" He looked at me and said, "Oh, no." He was so firm about it, like it was impossible that his father would have been nice.

Sometimes we'd spend the whole day organizing. I think the main purpose was to turn the compost pile, so that what's at the bottom comes to the top. It's what lots of artists do: you revisit your material.

But that's not what he said. What he said we were doing was organizing. Mostly what we were doing was taking some things that were in two boxes and putting them in one box, or things that were in one box and putting them in two boxes. We threw out very little. Every once in a while he'd say, "Oh, I don't want this," and once in a while he'd give me something that he didn't want, but mostly it was a kind of review, and it suited me. I liked doing it. I also don't throw things away. I know it would probably make some people very edgy to spend day after day picking up things and making decisions about them that never really get acted on, and then putting them back again. It was a combination of liking to look at the stuff and the process itself—it was soothing.

You could make suggestions, but not a lot of them, and you

had to flow with the whole thing, just move with him, with the slowness of time, which I liked.

Sometimes, just because of logistics, we'd all of a sudden be in the kitchen together, and it was very clear that he didn't have anything for me to do. It would make him edgy, and I knew not to ask him what I should do because he didn't like that. So I found that if I got quieter and quieter and calmer and calmer he'd start to forget I was there. It was an ability I worked on. It's one reason that photographs looking out the kitchen window or near the kitchen sink are so particular to me, because that was where I would stand sometimes for hours and literally try to dematerialize myself. I would make my presence lighter and lighter and lighter—

WILLARD: Two apparitions!

ROSEMAN: And I wondered, did I look different? I don't know. It didn't make me tired standing there. I mean, I'd stand there sometimes for hours, just looking out the window. It was a kind of meditation. And part of what I would do was literally to make my presence not felt. So it was a combination of my mind getting lighter and my mind trying to make my body lighter. I got very good at it. I should revisit it periodically now when I get tense because it's very freeing.

I wouldn't have been surprised if he'd bumped into me, though he never did.

WILLARD: Did you ever feel he was taking you for granted?

ROSEMAN: He wasn't easy. Sometimes it went really well. Sometimes I was very happy to be there. Other times he drove me crazy, especially the first year. I don't think he knew what he wanted our relationship to be. Sometimes he would treat me like a confidante and talk to me, not like someone who worked for him but like someone closer. And other times he was very abrupt, and very dismissive, and it hurt my feelings.

WILLARD: Did he talk a lot?

ROSEMAN: Little by little he talked more and more. At first it was very professional. He gave me my work, I had coffee breaks, I had lunch breaks. We never had them together, at least not the first month. It didn't take too long till he started joining me, and sometimes I would go into the kitchen and have my coffee break and my lunch, and he'd take naps or lie down. For lots of my lunches I ate peanuts and cheese. I think it may have had to do with what was in the house. And the fact that there were birds and squirrels outside, so there were always plenty of peanuts around. And I really enjoyed it. I would sometimes eat tons of peanuts and a big chunk of cheese. And that was my lunch.

WILLARD: And you didn't turn into a squirrel.

ROSEMAN: I didn't turn into a squirrel. And then little by little he started joining me. For breaks and for lunch. And sometimes we'd sit for a couple of hours and he would just talk. And sometimes he would take notes. He took notes all the time, as everyone knows, and he had all these dossiers and envelopes all over the place, with different categories. Sometimes in the envelopes there would be art reproductions or things that started to branch out from the initial impetus. Sometimes I'd say something and he'd write it over five times. I'd see him write it over and over again. He helped me hone my ability to read upside down. But his handwriting was very scribbly and very hard to read.

WILLARD: You said you took notes. But not in front of him.

ROSEMAN: I didn't take a lot of notes. I'm a disorganized person who has a desire to be organized. So my notes are very sporadic.

WILLARD: Obviously he was aware that you were taking photographs. How did he feel about that?

ROSEMAN: I've been taking photographs pretty regularly since I was thirteen. I got into the habit of carrying my camera all the time. So it wasn't unusual that I would have my camera with me when I went to his house for work. But at first I didn't take any pictures. I started by taking a picture of the yard or the house and at some point I showed him some pictures that were kind of relevant to him. And then he got used to me having my camera and periodically he would ask me to take a picture of something.

WILLARD: Something that he might use?

ROSEMAN: Yes. And then it evolved. For instance, he had me take pictures of food periodically. People would give him food; there was this really fancy birthday cake like a supermarket birthday cake with roses and white icing and stuff, and he handed it to me and said, "Oh, could you do something with this?" I took it out in the yard and I made some photos. One time he had this piece of sponge cake that was maybe a couple of months old so it had gotten rocklike, dried up and hard, like something petrified. And he said, "Oh, could you do something with this?" So I went out and took some pictures.

He had some flowers someone gave him, in the house, and they died. And he sent me out to do a series of photographs of this vase. It was a very fancy vase, crystal and silver. It was his mother's.

I did a whole series of photographs of pears. The pears were really intriguing. There was a front door and side back door, and a mudroom. The light in the mudroom was very beautiful. So one day I came in and there were these pears on the window sill. And they were very ordinary, pristine, three perfect pears in a soft light, and I just took a photo of them. If that had been it, it wouldn't have meant very much to me, because it was a pretty photograph, possibly too pretty. But over the next weeks these pears—sometimes there was one, sometimes there were three, they started to shrivel up. It was like this pear performance. And sometimes they'd be cut in quarters, and they had nails sticking out of them. He was doing this when I wasn't there.

WILLARD: Good heavens—crucified pears.

ROSEMAN: One time they were all shriveled up with the nails sticking up. They were really riveting to me. I took twenty photographs of this pear process. But we never talked about it. I didn't show him these photos.

WILLARD: It's a story. They're looking at each other, talking to each other.

ROSEMAN: They *are* narrative, but they're so elusive. And it's certainly about deterioration and time, but then there's this strange intervention. The nails are what really threw me. The first day I got there and the nails started to appear I went *wow.*

WILLARD: So you had already started the series when the nails appeared.

ROSEMAN: There must be at least four or five photographs before the nails.

WILLARD: You must have wondered each day what a new chapter would reveal.

ROSEMAN: Yes, and I think it's one reason that I took so many photographs. Because in another situation I probably wouldn't have photographed certain things. But because everything had this imbued quality everything started to look wonderful.

WILLARD: Did he know you were taking them?

ROSEMAN: No. I'd get there in the morning and take my coat off in the mudroom. I'd take my pear picture. And then I'd come in and we'd go about our business. We never talked about it. I never knew what was up exactly, and I think he didn't know I was documenting this pear thing, although other people theorize that he knew we were having this dance. Eventually it stopped.

WILLARD: How do you think Cornell was using those pears?

ROSEMAN: I don't really know. It seems to me it doesn't have to have an explicable purpose beyond the act itself. Sometimes things would happen that were played out as a kind of story or dance, none of it self-contained, because everything meant something to him, and everything was about his work, and everything was special. I mean, he was someone who used things in his work that were sometimes esoteric and sometimes ordinary, but in either case once his glance hit it, it was special. In the kitchen, other things would start to take on an evolving still life quality. He collected stamps. Sometimes I'd come in and there'd be different stamps stuck on the window in the kitchen. And then they'd come down, and other stamps would go up.

One thing about being there and knowing him and being with him is this: in how we respond to things we have a choice as to whether to keep our self-conscious coolness and our analytical ability or to go with something. To suspend disbelief. It's a kind of faith, in a sense. I wonder if I'm as capable of it now as I was then, but there was something about loving his work, being so thrilled to be there, and maybe being young, I gave myself up to this in a big way. Maybe that's another reason it worked so well.

So, for instance, a nail was not just a nail. Everything would take on this aura. And he would talk about things in a certain way, and his world—everything around him that he put his glance on that he incorporated into this fantasy or whatever you want to call it—took on a kind of specialness. And so I really got into it.

For example, outside in the yard there was a stone squirrel and a ceramic frog and these plaster rabbits, a big rabbit and baby rabbits. Then there's the whole history of his brother Robert's rabbit drawings. He told me once that James Thurber came over and really liked Robert's drawings. So I started to internalize some of that. These plaster rabbits, which are just junky plaster rabbits that come from some nursery, were the only plaster rabbits like these in the whole world. When I photographed those rabbits, I felt like I was photographing something rather extraordinary. I wonder what happened to those bunnies. I wonder if anybody saved them.

WILLARD: Can you tell me what it was like to work alongside Cornell in that basement studio?

ROSEMAN: One thing that always struck me, when we were down in the cellar, for instance, and we would be making these boxes, almost everything was kind of fraught with scarcity and not being obtainable any more. Even nails sometimes. We'd pick up nails and he'd say, "Oh, you can't get nails like this." And of course you could. He liked to make everything so—well, he seemed to be saying, I'm so lucky to have this particular nail. Everything became particularized. Sometimes he would pick something up and say, "This will have to do. Not that I'm compromising. But this will have to do."

And a lot of things were like that. Everything was scarce. The electric saw broke. So we talked about getting it fixed, and he talked about his brother-in-law fixing it. He would say, "Oh, manpower is very scarce." His brother-in-law lived on Long Island, and it would take a long time for him to get to it.

I'd say, "Well, do you want me to look into it and find someone to fix it?" This suggestion would not please him.

Other times I'd go out and buy frames for collages at the local frame store. The most ordinary frames. I'd just go out and get twenty of them. He'd stain them a little bit, he'd change them a little bit. The framing for the boxes—I think it was harder for him to go out and gather old wood to cut up for frames. Originally I think some of the forms for the boxes were found stuff, and then eventually he built them or had them made.

When I first started working for him, we worked on boxes that were around the studio. And then he sent me to the lumberyard with a box so they could copy it, because he figured he'd order a bunch. Sometimes I made new ones. On these new boxes he'd have old wood he had scavenged from demolition sites, and I'd cut them and miter them and make them into frames to go over these new boxes.

Sometimes he'd age them and sometimes he'd find them layered and aged enough. He had this one piece where he had three sides and he needed a fourth one, and my job was to replicate it. It was a lot of fun. I took this piece of wood and I just layered it and layered it and used different kinds of paint and filled in the cracks, and when I put it together, even I couldn't tell which was the piece I'd made. So I was very pleased with that little dance.

WILLARD: Can you look at a box of his and say, Yes, this is a box I worked on?

ROSEMAN: I'm not sure. They were made in such close series—a bunch of moon boxes, a bunch of constellation boxes. For some reason I didn't photograph the boxes I worked on. I don't even know which one I made the piece of wood on and probably will never know, and also partly because his dating was very vague. He didn't like this hierarchy of a certain period of work being thought better than others, and I know that there has to be a lot of guesswork in dating his work.

So I don't know. Which is strange. I remember some of the forms we worked on. I built a box within a box once for him. But there was a series of those. And this was twenty-five years ago.

One time he missed one of his boxes a great deal and he

showed me a reproduction of it and said, "Please make this for me." He'd sold it for a very small amount of money. He used to bemoan that a lot. "Oh, I shouldn't have sold that." He sold them for fifty bucks, a hundred bucks—this was a long time ago. This one box he wanted to have around. It was fun. I built this box from scratch. And then he signed it.

WILLARD: So he got very attached to some of the boxes.

ROSEMAN: Oh, he did. And by the time I worked for him, he had as much money as he needed which was not a lot. He didn't want a lot of money, so he sold just as much as he felt like. He didn't have any regular dealer at that point. A woman named Jane Wade would sell work for him; she worked out of her house and she took very low commissions.

Once in a while he would let people come over to buy some boxes, either because he had a history with them or through someone. But usually he'd like people to come over when I wasn't working, so in getting ready for someone coming over the next day when I wasn't going to be there we went around and hid things. "Let's hide these, let's hide these, let's hide these. Okay, we can show them these."

Every once in a while there'd be a lot of activity. There would be a whole bunch of people coming over. Once there was a really spiffy-looking French couple. They looked like movie stars, and they bought a box, and he had them make out a check to some children's charity. Sometimes he would sell things to give the money away, and sometimes he would sell things to live off the money, but he didn't like to sell them a whole lot.

He was very frugal. He kept tea bags and used them over and over again. He'd use a paper towel and then stick it up on a nail and use it again. Because he was so frugal he hardly put the heat on all winter. It was a very cold fall that first fall I worked for him, and I was cold all the time. He walked around a lot with this big heavy terrycloth blue bathrobe on, and sometimes he'd put it over his clothes, and then he'd put the gas burners on and stand in front of the stove to warm up.

Every once in a while his bathrobe would catch on fire. One time we were in the kitchen and the bathrobe caught on fire, and I had to put it out. And one time I came in, and the belt to his bathrobe was on the floor, looking like a partly burned cigarette. I didn't see the fire, but I saw the results of it.

And sometimes I took to standing in front of the stove for a little bit because I was cold. Eventually he'd say, "Are you cold?" I would say, "Yes," and he'd turn the heat up. I felt that was a turning point in our relationship.

WILLARD: Did you take many pictures of his studio?

ROSEMAN: I have a series of these studio pictures.

WILLARD: Good heavens, the place looks like organized chaos.

ROSEMAN: Oh, yes, there were all these boxes of materials, and then these partly done works. These are the shelves with frame and dowels and pieces of wood. The stuff he put in his boxes—shells, fancy little things—were over there.

WILLARD: How did he find the things he put in his boxes?

ROSEMAN: He mostly gathered them up. He'd go on expeditions. By the time I worked for him, a lot of the stuff was there already in the studio. In his work there is a dialogue between those kinds of things.

WILLARD: The shelves look so narrow—and all those old pipes . . .

ROSEMAN: It's just a cellar, very sparsely lit with hanging bulbs. This trunk was full of glorious boxes, just beautiful boxes, which were mostly hoarded. Sometimes I'd sit down there and look at those boxes.

WILLARD: So many books, and so many records. Did he listen to music when he was working?

ROSEMAN: He listened to music a lot. Sometimes when we were down there he'd put records on. Classical records, a lot of Chopin, Debussy. He liked the French composers. He liked Satie a lot. Some of the records were never unwrapped.

WILLARD: What's this picture with the sheets covering up the furniture?

ROSEMAN: That's what we did sometimes when company was coming and we wanted to make things neat. Things got draped, like in a house that is not being occupied. It was fun.

WILLARD: I notice that a lot of your photographs were taken in the kitchen.

ROSEMAN: I know from things I've read that when he was younger and his mother was around, he always worked in the kitchen, until he got his studio in the basement. But even when I was working for him, I have a feeling he worked a lot in the kitchen during the night, because sometimes I'd get there in the morning and there would be this whole worktable set up on the kitchen table. He was doing a series of Rorschach collage drawings. The kitchen was also a work area.

The kitchen was painted this wonderful blue. He was a young adult when it got painted. He had to go to the store, and he wanted the kitchen to be Giotto blue. He told me he was embarrassed to tell this to the paint store man—he thought it was kind of affected—so he said to the clerk, "My mother told me to ask for Giotto blue."

WILLARD: Looking at your photographs of the interior of the house, I never once wondered about the color.

ROSEMAN: The house was so dark inside that it *did* seem black and white. Here's another way of describing it. When I was in junior high school, sometimes my mother would stay up late and when I'd come home for lunch, she'd still be sleeping. So when I'd walk in the door with my key, the house had a kind of sleepy, dark, out-of-time-sequence feeling.

And that's what his house felt like. Eventually he gave me a key, and in the morning I'd let myself in. Sometimes he'd still be sleeping.

WILLARD: Did he use those glasses on the windowsill for boxes or medicine?

ROSEMAN: Those are for the little trinkets he would put in—a feather, or a stamp, or something. To keep it in view. This jar holds mucilage, that kid glue.

Then he had a calendar and a notepad and sometimes he'd

make these diagrams which he'd set up, and they were kind of like schedules but not schedules; they were reminders for him. Then there'd be titles of boxes he wanted to think about like *Penny Arcade* and *Hotel du Nord*. In the middle of all these other lists, there are shopping lists.

A photograph like this is about light, and it's about his place, and it's about surface, and it's about a certain time, but for me it's mostly about what it felt like to be in that kitchen on a certain day, and the way time and light are there. When I look at this photograph it brings back the place but even more, it brings back the way it felt. The way it felt to be there.

WILLARD: What's the story behind that sign? "Attention family and helpers, all valuables have been removed to storage vaults."

ROSEMAN: That's the alarm system. It was supposed to throw the robbers off. He couldn't just say, "Attention, robbers." That would give it away.

He had a bedroom upstairs, which I have a photo of, but lots of times he'd be sleeping on the downstairs daybed, and I'd come in, and sometimes I'd just tiptoe around for an hour or so till he woke up. Other times he'd be clearly bustling around. I think he probably had sporadic hours, so sometimes he'd get up and work in the middle of the night. And then he took naps during the day. Sometimes when we were working, he would say, "Keep yourself busy. I'm going to go take a nap."

Here's the photo of his bedroom. It's very monk-like, cell-like.

WILLARD: I can imagine him making up his bed in that minimal room.

ROSEMAN: And you have this towel, and this sheet, and the curtains. You know how I go crazy for drapery.

WILLARD: What a traditional dresser.

ROSEMAN: That's partly because this house was not furnished by him. So there are all these vestiges of an older family style. Very little was changed. For instance, one time we were standing in one of the rooms, and he looked at the wall and up toward the ceiling. Everything needed to be painted. He saw a crack in the paint and said, "Oh, my God." Like he'd never seen it before. And then he snapped out of it.

WILLARD: What did the outside of the house look like? And the yard?

ROSEMAN: It was a very regular sort of Dutch gambrel 1920s row house. His house and the one on the left were unaltered. But they all had these little square backyards. The backyard was very contained. I was there for only three Christmases, I think, and he would not throw the Christmas trees away for a long time. At one point we had two or three Christmas trees in the yard in different states of decay with a little bit of glitter and foil on them. And when the wreath came off the door, it went out to the backyard and lived there for awhile. A lot of things became characters, an extension of a world you can know and affect.

Behind the yard was a garden apartment complex. Everyone talks about this, but certainly there was something about the heightened specialness of him and the house in this absolutely regular environment which is unavoidable. The person who owns and lives in the house now organizes children's birthday parties for a living.

WILLARD: How did Cornell get on with the neighbors?

ROSEMAN: He talked to the neighbors on both sides, and they seemed to know he was an artist. I know he gave some work to the neighbor on one side.

WILLARD: Though I've never set foot in the house or the yard, I do get a feeling for the place. I think the artist in his own setting is one of the subjects you're dealing with.

ROSEMAN: I think it's the major subject.

WILLARD: Which is why your photographs give me a portrait of Cornell that's unlike any I've ever seen. I still don't know how you managed to take any candid pictures of him.

ROSEMAN: The pictures I usually took are interactive. When he was posing for me, sometimes it was my idea and sometimes it was his idea. I was very well aware, though we were comfortable with each other, that he didn't like to be photographed all that much. He was reticent, and sometimes I knew if I made one wrong move he'd bolt, because his moods would go up and down very quickly.

They were nice moments, relaxed and intimate in a certain way, and the whole time I'm trying not to blow it, by just feeling what the parameters were, what I could ask him to do, how long it could go on, how calm to be. How invisible I could be.

In some of these sessions he was extremely relaxed and cooperative. It would be for me as much of a communing or being close as anything else we did, because I felt he was giving over to me something that he didn't easily give.

WILLARD: He doesn't look as if he's posing.

ROSEMAN: He never quite looked at you very often anyway, so in all the pictures he's slightly looking down. His eyes were very inset in his head, and in shadow sometimes. Very rarely did he look at the camera, which felt like a kind of shyness. Someone did ask me if he was shy and I couldn't answer, because "shy" doesn't seem like the right word. I'm not sure if "shy" explains it.

Sometimes he became almost unaware that I was photographing him in the middle of photographing him. Which was very nice.

WILLARD: Did he like the ones you took of him?

ROSEMAN: The most he did was not mind some. He would never go so far as to say he liked it. He liked other photos that I took, and sometimes he used them in collages. But pictures of himself he wouldn't respond to in the same way. Either he was horrified or he didn't have much of a reaction.

WILLARD: How long had you been working with him when you took these photographs?

ROSEMAN: 1971 seems to me the most active period of photographing him. I have none of him from '69, the first year, which isn't surprising. One of my favorite set of photos he hated—he shuddered when he saw them.

WILLARD: With the mirrors and corners and reflections in your pictures of him, he becomes a figure in his own work. You found the right title for your show: "Inside the Box: A Photographic

Portrait of Joseph Cornell." You've really created a picture of him from inside the box.

ROSEMAN: Actually Cathy thought of the title. The show is about being inside the box, inside his head, inside my head.

WILLARD: That makes the pictures different from other photographs of Cornell I've seen.

ROSEMAN: One of the differences might be this: taking those pictures was part of my everyday life at that moment, as well as part of his. It's not like I had an appointment with him and had to arrive at his house at three o'clock and take a series of photos. They were done in the fabric of going about our business.

WILLARD: Did Cornell ever do any teaching?

ROSEMAN: He visited a couple of classes at Queens College. He didn't really teach. But he had all these ideas and schemes. Some of them were about a kind of floating classroom for making Cornell boxes. Sometimes we'd do a box or part of a box, and he'd say, "Oh, good, we can use that for an example for schools." And so we'd put it aside. Sometimes the idea was about having people come in and run a school, sometimes it was about going out to a school. But it was always vague, and it always seemed to be about making Cornell boxes.

One time he said to me, "Make me a box [in one of his forms] that is not one of my boxes but your response to it, and we could use that for teaching." So I made a box. I went home and built this whole box with fish and glitter and mirrors and stuff—it was a lot of fun—and then I brought it to him, and he said, "Okay, good." And he put it aside.

WILLARD: What happened to that box?

ROSEMAN: I've no idea. I've never seen it again. Unlike some of the others I worked on, I would recognize that box, because I made it. It was in a sense commissioned, a commission for some vague client. He was the client but the real client was this idea of a kind of teaching apparatus. My box was a way to show how someone might make a Cornell box who wasn't Cornell but could bring their own thing into it. It would go in and out of our conversation over the years. Sometimes he'd ask me for ideas so we could push forward.

But he didn't really want them. The few times I would broach anything like that, it wouldn't make him happy at all. It was just a kind of thinking out loud, which I had to get used to: the difference between what was really being asked of me and what was being asked but not wanted at all.

There was a lot of that. Sometimes he wouldn't be talking to me particularly, he would just be musing out loud. It might have gotten triggered because I was there, and then we'd disconnect and reconnect. Sometimes he would talk directly to me about some of these projects, and at a certain point it all became very abstract. Then it was like music, just something washing over me that was very pleasant.

WILLARD: It doesn't sound like conversation as most people know it. And yet it's what I would imagine happening in this house. Getting ready for the show, going through the photographs, do you feel you've stepped back into that time and place?

ROSEMAN: It's a compression of time for me. This is an old body of work and now it's become a new body of work, because I've had to revisit it and reassess the images. There's the connection between my present and that part of my life twenty-five years ago, and there's the connection with him. He really dates back to the early part of the century, so I feel like it's made my arm longer, reaching in and out of time. You look at people's biographies, their birth and death dates, and you think about people who were born in the middle of a century and then died in the middle of the next century, or people who were born at the end of one century and lived through most of the next century, or people who were born and lived only twenty years. You think about that and all the ripples that go flowing back from that. Something about this project has woven those ripples together for me.

Recently I found a letter from him. I was away in Massachusetts, and he said how he missed my eye and my camera. You remember some things, you forget some things. It was almost like he'd said it today.

Not by Bread Alone:
A Portrait of Simone Levy

⟡

WHEN A SMALL STORE called La Belle Chocolatière moved into the town of Poughkeepsie, one block away from Vassar College, it did not take people long to discover reasons for stopping there other than the coffee, bread, and exquisite desserts and chocolates advertised on the placard in the window. The postal clerk and the Korean couple who own the dry cleaners next door come for coffee breaks and conversation. Students from the college drop in for French rolls and croissants and stay to practice their French, Hebrew, or Arabic with Simone Levy, the Moroccan-born wife of the master pastry chef, Alain, who also teaches the baker's art to aspiring chefs at the Culinary Institute of America in Hyde Park.

Though she stands behind the counter and waits on customers, anyone who engages Simone in conversation soon discovers that her experience and her knowledge reach far beyond that little shop. Customers who see no further than the work she performs here can hardly imagine the very different kinds of specialized jobs she has done, for which she is highly qualified.

Simone Levy was born in Morocco, but fled after the French Protectorate ended in 1956. "The Moroccan people were getting rid of the French. The king was in exile, in Madagascar. At the same time the Sinai war was going on, and the Algerian war. All of these conflicts didn't help the Jewish people in Morocco. We left in the sixties, because we knew we couldn't leave after they closed the border. One by one, we left. When I left, I was fifteen."

She traveled through Gibralter to Marseilles, and eventually settled in Israel, where she took a job working in the dining room at the Hilton in Tel Aviv. There she met and married Alain, the pastry chef of the hotel. They moved to Switzerland, where their three children were born, then to Israel and to France, dividing their time between Strasbourg and Paris. In 1976 they emigrated to Canada. Six years later they arrived in the United States.

I come to La Belle Chocolatière for coffee, for bread, and for stories about Simone Levy's family. The stories help me understand why she has worked so successfully at jobs as diverse as a masseuse, a make-up artist, and a caterer with an extraordinary knowledge of food and its preparation. But since nobody can tell those stories better than Simone, I shall let her speak for herself.

A Birth and a Blessing

I was born in a carriage with horses, like those in Central Park. People in Morocco rarely went to the hospital; they were born at home. But my father didn't believe in that. He believed in going to the hospital. My mother took the carriage—we didn't have a car—and the driver drove so fast he nearly ran the horse to death. At midnight, like Cinderella, I was born. I weighed six kilos, and I had long hair. And the lady who was with my mother said. "God bless, Holy God, God bless, Holy God, she is going to travel all her life." And it's true. I *have* traveled all my life.

My mother used to say. "I wish you to have children who are born as fast as you were born." She blessed me with that. And she said, "You were so nice, just eating and sleeping." Well, I had the same thing with my children. If I hadn't gone to the hospital on time, I would have had them on the road, too.

The Godmother and Her Seven Daughters

My mother's godmother had seven daughters. Because none of the seven daughters had children of their own, they pampered my mother like a queen. They took her to school and brought her back; she used to say she never had to carry her own schoolbag.

Every day she had a massage with oil on her body, and she had a seamstress come every week at home to do her clothes. Her name was Luna, and she was beautiful. The seven daughters used to put special oils on her hair. There is a root we have in Morocco, called mandragora. It has the power to enhance the growth of the hair and the thickness. My mother had such long hair that she used to tell me, "Do you see those marks on the floor? When my hair reached to the floor, I would step on it. Those marks are from stepping on my hair." We used to braid her hair. We couldn't do one braid. We had to do two.

She was a teacher. She taught history and French literature. And when she had twins she became a kindergarten teacher (we were the twins!) so she could be with them at school. That's one thing my father wanted, for her to be with the children. She took them every day to school with her and brought them home. She was a very good mother.

The Grandmother Who Saw the Light of God

Nahmany was my name before I was married. My great-grandfather and my grandfather were Cabalists. The Cabalists study the Zohar, the mystical Book of Splendor. They know all the laws— diet, astrology, astronomy, nutrition, food, medicine, everything. You know, there are 920 signs which show you how to recognize a person who is dying. My grandfather could do that. My father, too.

According to Jewish law, the sick and the dying are the holiest to deal with, because they are closest to God, and because you must have compassion to deal with them. You must be holy yourself to do this; you cannot cheat or do other things forbidden by law.

When my grandmother died, she knew what was happening to her. One Friday afternoon she was sleepy. We had a big house, with a courtyard and tiles, and she came out and told my mother, "Luna, do you see this beautiful garden and trees? Oh, I feel so restless in my body." And then she said, "Look at this light coming from the sky." She was seeing the *shekhina,* the radiant light of God. She was seeing her future. She said to my mother, "Is my son here?" And my mother said, "Yes, he will come soon." My grandmother kept asking for him. And I remember my mother said, "You keep asking for him the whole day. It's like you're the only one who has a son."

Then she told my mother, "When he comes, ask him to wash his hands and cut his nails. Then I will be ready." In Jewish law, nails are not clean, not pure. When my father stepped in, he said, "How is Mom?" and my mother said, "Okay." He asked, in French, if she needed anything. And my grandmother, who did not speak French, replied, "I won't need anything today." My mother brought her a cup of soup, and she lay down. And in a few seconds—well, you know.

She was a very nice lady. When I came home, she would say, "Go the drawer of my buffet, and open it. There is something for you." There would be dates and nuts in it. No candy. She didn't believe in candy.

Every day she would do her bread and bring it to us, because she believed the wheat had more elements and was more complete than any other cereal. She never bought flour. She'd buy the wheat, take her time to clean it, and then break it by hand to a flour, and make the bread. She was so cautious she never bought anything from the outside, not even sugar. She sweetened her cooking with dates. She would eat nothing from the fridge. Everything had to be prepared totally according to Jewish law.

Both of my grandmothers knew about food and medicine. Through food she even learned to heal. She knew about every herb; she knew how to use thyme and fennel. She was a very strong woman.

The Work of the Baker: One by One, with One Hand.

It says on this matzoh box that these matzohs were baked eighteen minutes after the wheat was harvested. The wheat has to be cut when there is no dew, because of the possibility of fermentation. The person who grinds the wheat has to clean everything and make sure there is nothing left inside, and of course the rabbi checks and blesses it, and then they grind the flour, and from this time they have only eighteen minutes to do the baking. Otherwise, it becomes fermented.

My grandmother used to do all this by herself. She wouldn't trust anything made by anybody else. She had the oven outside, and she would make the matzohs one by one. With one hand. That is the custom.

Work of Preparing Food: From Chicken to Eggplant

In Morocco, everybody is used to going to the market every day. When you go to the market, you see the chickens in cages, screaming. You choose the chicken live. And you tell the man, "That's the one I want," and he puts your name on the feet, and when you come back, your chicken is cleaned and slaughtered. Slaughtered on the spot. You have everything in the market. Even the fish is fresh.

At the market, we could buy all the fruits and vegetables in season. We like to candy them—carrots, mandarin oranges, grapes, raisins and walnuts together, and eggplant. The eggplant is called the king of vegetables. When you candy the eggplant, it comes out deep purple. You have to pick them, cook them, and put them in water for twenty-four hours, and you must change the water, to take out the bitterness. Next, you cook the eggplant in water, adding an amount of sugar equal to the weight of the vegetable, and pieces of clove and sticks of cinnamon. You cook it until the sugar becomes candy. We serve candied eggplant for a dessert when people come over to visit. It's like an ornament, really. It looks beautiful.

When I do the strawberries for jam, I want the whole berry to stay red and not to turn dark. You prepare the sugar and cook it, and one degree before the sugar candies, you throw your strawberry in. That's all. And they stay red forever.

The Work of the Hands: On Learning Massage

When I was little the neighborhood children would ask me to massage their feet. They used to tell me that I had good hands, but I thought it was just because they wanted me to do it. I did massage for all the neighbors. For my father too. When I was in Switzerland, I was studying biology, and after I had my children, I changed to physical therapy. And I started working for a company that made products for the body. And they asked me if I wanted to use the products and tell them the results.

So I took some classes on how to do facials and ended up studying make-up. I kept studying for a year. Then we went to Canada. And a friend of mine there said, "I want to become a beautician. Let's go to school." The Canadian government was paying anyone who went to school 250 a week. So I went back to school and took some biology classes to see if I could follow it. After three months they told me I could not stay, I knew too much. So I applied to a school for doing facials and I went there with my friend in Montreal. There is no age limit to learning. And I started to work.

My friend used to tell me, "When you give a facial, it is special." When I left Canada, I gave her the name of another friend who could do facials, and one day she called and said, "Simone, I tried. It is not the same." So I believe there is something special about my hands. And I feel it when I do the massage. My hand won't stop. As long as the person needs it, I can see what part needs work.

A bony hand is not good for massage. It has to be muscle, nice and soft.

The Work of the Face: On Learning Make-up

It starts with basic makeup, which is make-up for the daytime. You have to learn the color, the chemistry, and the technique of doing the make-up itself. We went to the factory to learn where the colors and textures came from. You study morphology, and the different colors of eyes and skin. You learn how to shape eyebrows, and how to mix and apply all the foundations. You should not be able to see that the person has foundation on her skin. And even before you apply it, you have to see if the person has wrinkles or some feature she wants to hide. Make-up is much more complicated than most people think.

After you have applied the foundation, you put on the rice powder, which fixes it, and then you start with the eye shadow, according to what the person will wear or what fits the color of her eyes. Then you do the cheeks and the lips. That's the day make-up.

Then you learn the night make-up. The last one you learn is theater make-up. This includes all kinds of clowns, and characters from different centuries and races. When we learned to make the different kinds of beards, we had to stick them on, hair by hair. We had to try it on ourselves, because it involved glue, and nobody wants to have glue on his face.

I tell people, there are many ways you can help your skin. Relaxation is very important. If you are mean, it shows in your face.

The Wedding

It is customary before the wedding to wear the traditional wedding dress on the henna night, when there's food and dancing the night before the wedding, even if she plans to wear a white dress for the ceremony. The henna dress is burgundy velvet, thickly made, with lots of gold embroidery. Sleeves cannot be sewn in because the fabric is so thick, so the bride wears a sheer blouse under it with see-through sleeves. She wears a gold belt with all kinds of stones, and a crown. It is a dress fit for a queen.

We don't do showers, we have a party to show the trousseau. The bride shows all the embroidery and the work she has made with her hands. The wedding is a seven days' celebration. And the oldest woman cooks for the whole day.

The Curfew

When the Moroccan people wanted to get rid of the French, we had a curfew. I remember how neighbors would come over, and we would sit and hear stories or play cards together. That's how people met each other. If a woman was pregnant, people brought her food, everybody brought her a plate. It was the same with everything. We shared the work. When a woman had a baby, everybody would come to help the mother. We all lived together, and that's how people met each other. The synagogue was close, we could walk to it. We were not permitted to drive. We walked everywhere. We had everything.

We had each other.

Eden Revisited

THE FIRST GARDEN I never saw was the Garden of Eden. Nevertheless, I knew it had no winter, no mosquitoes, no weeds, no gypsy moths, and no root borers. What a pity that the first occupants of that garden had nothing to do with the planning and the making of it. The serpent was the instrument of the Fall but not, I think, the cause of it. Eve was bored.

If Adam and Eve had been set down in Stanley Kunitz's garden in Provincetown, their story might have ended differently. Stanley could have said to them, "I never am absent from the garden, even when I'm away from it."[1] He would have told them how his garden was born on a patch of land as bare as the earth on the first day of creation, and how he gathered old doors and boards to keep the drifting sand from swamping it. He would have told them how for the sake of the soil he harvested kelp and rockweed, sometimes as many as six bags a day, washed up on the beaches at the far end of the Cape, and he would have shown them how terracing keeps the soil in place. He would told them about weather and seasons, seed time and harvest, and what it's like to carry the marvelous burden of living in time. He would say,

I can scarcely wait till tomorrow
when a new life begins for me,
as it does each day,
as it does each day.[2]

When Adam and Eve noticed the winding paths in his garden, he would have shown them how to walk the same path day after day yet never take the same journey twice. When they admired his anemones and cosmos and late-blooming roses, he would have shown them the snakes, and invited them to stroke "the fine dry grit of their skins."[3] He might have even asked them to consider the garden from the snakes' point of view and given Adam and Eve their first lesson in negative capability.

And finally they would understand what Stanley knows so well, that his garden and the making of it is a kind of poem, which depends for its life on both what you see and what you do not see. Many years ago I heard Stanley tell the story of a couple who were visiting Provincetown and arrived at the garden in which Stanley was, at that moment, weeding and planting.

They asked him a question: is the poet in? Stanley replied, No, the poet is out today. Stanley's eye and heart miss nothing: the large absence of a cherry tree, the small courage of the hornworm, otherwise known as the larva of the hawk moth. It's a short step from Stanley's sympathy for the hornworm to Blake's sympathy for the glowworm and the housefly. The poem, "Hornworm: Autumn Lamentation, " is also one possible answer to a question posed in the last lines of Theodore Roethke's poem, "Slug," in which the poet asks the slug, "But as for you, most odious / Would Blake call you holy?"

HORNWORM: AUTUMN LAMENTATION

Since that first morning when I crawled
into the world, a naked grubby thing,
and found the world unkind,
my dearest faith has been that this
is but a trial: I shall be changed.
In my imaginings I have already spent
my brooding winter underground,
unfolded silky powdered wings, and climbed
into the air, free as a puff of cloud
to sail over the steaming fields,

alighting anywhere I pleased,
thrusting into deep tubular flowers.

It is not so: there may be nectar
in those cups, but not for me.
All day, all night, I carry on my back
embedded in my flesh, two rows
of little white cocoons,
so neatly stacked
they look like eggs in a crate.
And I am eaten half away.

If I can gather strength enough
I'll try to burrow under a stone
and spin myself a purse
in which to sleep away the cold;
though when the sun kisses the earth
again, I know I won't be there.

Instead, out of my chrysalis
will break, like robbers from a tomb,
a swarm of parasitic flies,
leaving my wasted husk behind.

Sir, you with the red snippers
in your hand, hovering over me,
casting your shadow, I greet you,
whether you come as an angel of death
or of mercy. But tell me,
before you choose to slice me in two:
Who can understand the ways
of the Great Worm in the Sky?[4]

NOTES

1. Stanley Kunitz, *The Wild Braid* (New York: Norton, 2005), p. 62.

2. Stanley Kunitz, "The Round," *The Collected Poems* (New York: Norton, 2002), p. 237.

3. Stanley Kunitz, "The Snakes of September," *The Wild Braid* (New York: Norton, 2005), p. 56.

4. Stanley Kunitz, "Autumn Lamentation," *The Collected Poems* (New York: Norton, 2002), pp. 259–60.

Sources

From the Ancestors

THE FIRST TIME I heard the word *rural* it was part of an address, Rural Delivery #3. The mailbox on that route was our mailbox, silver with a red flag hinged to the right side, and it stood beside a dozen other mailboxes on a dirt road in Stoney Lake, Michigan. The door, hinged at the bottom, was shaped like a church window and it never did shut tightly. One summer when the mail was sparse, a colony of wasps built a small nest inside, at the far end of the box. They left us alone and we left them alone to make, cell by cell, one of those beautiful nests that when hanging from a tree look like a sleeping thunderstorm.

Since that time I have seen many similar mailboxes in front of houses with lawns and paved roads and station wagons, all within easy driving distance of a shopping mall. Where does the boundary between city lives end and rural lives start? Imagine, for a moment, our solar system, and let the sun stand for life in the city. Let Mercury and Venus, the planets nearest the sun, stand for life in the suburbs. Let Earth, Mars, and Jupiter point to life in the country, with access to small towns, thinning out toward farmlands, Uranus and Neptune and the newly demoted dwarf planet, Pluto, those communities most distant from the city. Rural for me is somewhere between Earth and Pluto.

The dirt road that wound through the village of Stoney Lake and connected all our lives ended two doors down from our house. The lake, a hundred feet deep in the middle and a mile across, was almost never out of our sight. The opposite shore was sparsely settled with birch trees and cows. On the far horizon loomed a gravel pit, where many of the men from the area worked. During the summer, we children could play Red Rover, Red Rover in the road in front of our house till ten o'clock at night without seeing a single car. In the evening most of the fathers were off fishing or drinking; most of the mothers gathered in each other's front yards to chat, and when darkness came on, all that could be seen of them was the glowing tips of their cigarettes, though their voices kept on braiding and unbraiding in a comforting sort of way.

Later, much later, when the bars in the nearby towns closed, the men would come home. From my bedroom window I watched the man across the street drag his wife by the hair down the front steps of their house while the little girl I had been playing with only a few hours before hung on his belt screaming, "Don't hurt my mother! Don't hurt my mother!"

The next day, the men would get up as usual and go to work. In the sleepy sunlit morning, no one ever mentioned the violence that happened only at night, and the girl and I played together as if it had never happened at all. We played Tarzan and Jane in a jungle of oak and hickory and sassafras until we quarreled, because we both wanted to be Tarzan. Sometimes my sister and I played Moses in the Bulrushes with the rubber doll she had gotten as a reward for losing her tonsils, or we built stone castles under the water, swimming over the fish nests with great stones in our hands and placing them in a circle within a circle within a circle.

Lake water ran from the faucets of the houses, but we could not drink that water. Every morning my sister or I would lift the empty bucket from the top of the stove and walk half a block down the road to the pump for the water we would use all day. You had to wake the water; if you were its first visitor before breakfast, you could not hurry its journey from mineral darkness to sunlight. The pump stood on a wooden platform; if you pressed your ear to the gaps between the slats, you could hear the water singing in the well below.

The only store in Stoney Lake was a gas station that sold bread, milk, Coca-Cola, Lucky Strikes, hooks and bobbers for the fishermen, and tiny wax bottles filled with sweet colored syrup. Two miles away was the village of Oxford, which had sidewalks on both sides of the paved streets, a school and a library and a park with a bandstand and a weekly newspaper that occasionally featured the school lunch menu on the front page, along with a plea for news. Since my father was teaching summer school in Ann Arbor and my mother did not drive, we had the use of the car only on weekends, and a trip into town was rare. When my sister and I murmured about the lack of a Stoney Lake newspaper, our mother said, "You want a newspaper? Start your own."

So we did.

To gather the news, I would go from house to house with my notebook and pencil, knocking on doors, and to the person who opened the door I would say, "Has anything happened in this house?" Whatever I heard, I wrote it down. When we had enough news, my mother would sift through it and cut out anything that sounded like gossip. After my sister had written out the news with a special carbon pen, we ran off the newspaper on the wet face of a hectograph press, hung the sheets up in the living room to dry, and passed them out free.

And what did I learn as a writer from watching and listening to the lives of rural people? That you have to be part of the community to learn their stories, but only when you've left the community do you truly understand why they are worth saving.

When my grandmother lived with us in Ann Arbor, I was in high school and knew I wanted to be a writer. Grandmother's schooling had ended with eighth grade; the rural school took her no farther, and I knew my life would be very different from hers. My father was a teacher, not a farmer, and my parents would send me to college. Not till many years later did I turn to oral history as a way of coming to know what life was like for my grandmother in Deep River, Iowa. I had visited Deep River as a child, heard the family stories, and never forgot what wonderful storytellers lived there. Now they were elderly and some of them were in poor health. Who would save these stories of a way of life passing if I didn't? My sister and I traveled to Iowa with a tape recorder and asked the relatives to tell us again: what was your life on these farms when you were a child?

As we listened to their answers—and their answers were almost always stories—I thought of how their values had been passed on to my mother, and how many of those values she had passed on to me. Our mother had her own method of handing down the family lore beyond the simple telling of tales around the kitchen table. The week before Christmas, presents from friends and relatives, along with those we had made for our parents, would begin to accumulate under the tree. But not until Christmas Eve did the two gifts we most eagerly anticipated make their appearance. They were always wrapped, and the card on each package read, "From the ancestors." Inside would be something we had known all our lives: a carved spoon, a dipper for pulling the cream from the top of a bottle of unhomogenized milk, a tea strainer. Hand-me-downs from the dead, some of whom we'd met in our grandmother's stories and some whose names were lost to us. This was my mother's way of saying, "Someday you will be an ancestor and someday a child will hold this present and ask for your story."

I believe the power of objects to bind us to the past is especially strong in rural families because so many things in common use are handmade or adapted to a particular need. One of my great aunts lived all her life on the farm in Deep River, but only after her death did her children find the box of ancestor presents she had saved for them. She understood that children of a later generation would look at the ordinary implements she'd used and ask, "What on earth was this for?" So she wrote out descriptions of how she had used them on tiny sheets of notebook paper and fastened them with rubber bands to every object in that box:

This is the old husking peg that Dad fixed smaller to fit my hand when I used to help him husk corn the first year we were married and other years later, when the kids helped husk too, or the smaller ones rode in the wagon. I would get up early and put a chicken in the oil-stove oven and have the potatoes peeled and bread all baked ready in the big stone jar in the pantry. Butter churned and canned fruit in the basement I could open quick so we could hurry back to the field, then wash all those dishes at night. I made Aunt Annie's nice dresses over for the girls and I made the boys' everyday shirts and coveralls when they were small. Sat up many nights darning stockings and sacks or making comforters to keep everyone warm in the cold winters. Always was the first one up in the morning and started the fires and got breakfast ready. Those were the happy days when I had all my children near.

Is it a habit of all rural families or only mine never to throw anything away that you might find a use for? A few years ago when I was visiting my uncle in Guernsey, Iowa, he showed me a cyclone shelter he had built from a section of old sewer pipe that a local construction company had thrown away. It had the convenience of standing above ground, he explained, and it was tall enough to hold his whole family, including the grandchildren. From an old combine he'd built a replica of a World War I cannon named Big Bertha. He kept both of these in the front yard where other people have birdbaths. And he remembered how once upon a time anything you could not make—a bolt of cloth, a barrel of crackers—could be shipped by train from Chicago (Sears Roebuck) and picked up at the depot.

I didn't tell him that my mother had already taught me by her example to believe that what you need is right under your nose, and if you really need something you can find a way to make it. You should go to the store only as a last resort.

Even though we lived in Ann Arbor, where clothing shops abound, my mother still ordered many of our clothes from Sears Roebuck, just as her relatives in Iowa did, and she hired a dressmaker to teach me how to sew my own clothes so that I would not be subject to the whims of fashion. Let me tell you a little about this dressmaker. Her name was Ella. When she was much younger, Ella had asked my grandfather to cure her arthritis. My grandfather was an osteopath who had healing in his hands and goodness in his heart. If a patient was short on cash, he would accept payment in goods or services. One of his patients paid with him with watercolors of pallid floral arrangements and still lifes that nobody admired. Ella paid for her osteopathic treatments by sewing for the family, and after my mother grew up, she went on sewing for the next two generations. When Ella taught me to sew, she did not realize that she was also teaching me about good craftsmanship, whether the object at hand was a seam on a dress or a line in a poem.

I didn't realize how deeply I carried in my genes the lessons my mother had learned from her mother until the day my son, who was six years old, saw a video game in the window of a toy store and turned to me and said, "Mom, can you make me one of those?"

This streak of self-sufficiency, plus the strong sense of family, shapes the environment both of rural people and of their descendants. Though we lived in a university town, we had few paintings in our house, except those I made and those we had been given, including the anemic still lifes that my grandfather had accepted as payment for his osteopathic treatments.

Far more important than paintings were photographs. Family photographs. Every wall was covered with them. Nestled among the photographs hung important family documents, mostly diplomas framed in black frames from the dime store. All the years I was growing up, we especially revered one document, dated 1881, handwritten—the script was beautiful and the signature an elegant flourish—in a German dialect none of us could read, not even my grandmother, though she grew up speaking German, and both my father and I had studied it in school. But what did the content matter? Because it was clearly a present from the ancestors, it occupied a place of honor in our house.

One day a family friend, a professor in the Germanic Languages Department at the University, was visiting, and my mother asked if he would look at the document. Perhaps he could help us decode it. The professor studied it gravely, then turned to my mother.

"It certifies that Karl Wiedow's fourteen cows have been vaccinated against cowpox. And it is signed by the veterinarian."

My mother's disappointment was brief. We'd lived with it for so long that she could not imagine taking it down now, and so there it stayed, along with the diplomas and the photographs of children and grandchildren sitting patiently in the photographer's studio. To have no photograph of your ancestors, no enduring evidence of a face or gesture—what a catastrophe! When my father, an amateur photographer (who grew up to be a chemist), was a teenager in the small town of Union City, Michigan, he was occasionally called to make a portrait of someone who had lived without ever having been photographed. My father would tie his tripod, camera, and focusing cloth to his bicycle and pedal out into the country to take what would be the only existing portrait of the deceased, laid out in the parlor before the coffin lid shut him or her into that dark box from which no images emerge.

Sometimes my mother's friends would talk about remodeling or repainting their living rooms or bedrooms or kitchens. They spoke of interior decorators coming to their homes with plans, color charts, and swatches of fabric. My mother listened, half amused, half bewildered. The interior of your house was an extension of the family and a preserver of its values; how could an outsider with color charts and swatches possibly know what we would want? And why would we want new chairs and tables that matched but had never belonged to anybody else, sterile desks and china cabinets attended by no memories and hiding no stories? When I revisited the farmhouses of my relatives, I understood why our house in Ann Arbor looked the way it did. Our house had many more books than their houses and bigger closets and more of them. But the rationale for decorating was the same. And when I close my eyes and see myself in the little house looking out over Stoney Lake, I see my mother standing on a card table, painting the living room ceiling yellow and pressing decals of an ivy design on the rafters to make us believe that light from a garden just beyond our sight was watching over us and shining into that dark room.

An Ode to the Pantry

My Dear Professor Cupboard,

Oh, marvelous cupboard, keeper of our canned vegetables and soups behind your wooden doors under the counter in my mother's kitchen! I wonder if you still remember me. It was you who taught me the beauty of letters and their power to make words. While my mother baked the pecan loaves that my father loved (he was, you will recall, a vegetarian), I sat on the floor and opened those doors as I would later open the covers of books. You were my first primer. Under the cheerful paintings of yams, peas, beets, and green beans on the labels of cans, I studied the names printed above them. Dear Professor Cupboard, you taught me to read.

And to the spice family crammed into the little balcony over the stove, thank you. Your glass bottles, uniform in size, hid your secrets. Cinnamon was a saucy woman, ginger a jolly man. I thank you for the fragrance you gave my education.

A bouquet of thanks to the troupe of implements kept in a big drawer next to the sink. I was your dramaturge, I gave you my stories and you acted them out on the kitchen table. And what a cast! What other stage designer enjoys an ancient toaster that hides its electrical coils behind two doors and knows nothing of toast that pops up on command? What other theater is graced by a silver ball tea strainer twinkling on a slender chain like a porous planet? Or a juice strainer with cobweb-colored mesh, no bigger than a finch's nest? Or two pressure cooker tops, as round and cunning as stainless steel checkers? Or a long-handled spoon that bends and tangles with every fork it meets? For all the afternoons you entertained me, I thank you.

Or was it I who entertained you?

Last of all, I thank those who came into our kitchen from other houses and earlier times. The earthen crocks and Mason jars. The cream dipper for unhomogenized milk, sleek as the casing for a silver bullet. My grandmother's cookie cutters taught me to love shadows. My great-grandmother's corn bread pan, with its ten hollow molds shaped like ears of corn, taught me the use of emptiness.

I honor the implements my ancestors left behind: obsolete, curious, and too beloved to throw away.

The Cookies of Fortune

THE NIGHT BEFORE MY last class of the year, I am sitting at the dining room table with a pair of tweezers in my right hand and a fortune cookie in my left, extracting the fortune like the nerve in a bad tooth. In the college catalogue, the class is called English 217: Verse Writing. On dark winter mornings, the students arrive with coffee cups in their hands, and a single glance tells me who has stayed up too late studying for an exam or writing a paper.

Not until I stood on the other side of the desk did I realize that in the eternal present of the classroom the teacher sees every whisper, every frown, every struggle to overcome the effects of an all-nighter. On the last day, I bring in a pot of tea, a stack of paper cups, and fortune cookies. My students are mostly sophomores and juniors; they are the most promising group of poets I've ever taught, and miraculously they all seem to like one another.

I've fallen in love with all ten of them.

What fortunes can my ten young poets hope for? In the last three weeks before the end of the semester, two of them learned their parents were getting a divorce, one was told she had a new stepmother, one fretted over a younger brother with a serious illness.

I come from a long line of women who believed it was unwise to walk under a ladder, break a mirror, or open an umbrella in the house. When my mother spilled salt at the dinner table, she threw a pinch of it into the fire or over her left shoulder. Once a year, my great-grandmother would go down to the river near her farm to fill a bottle with "holy water," which had to be dipped from a running stream before sunrise on Easter morning.

I knew what these women say. Why leave their fortunes to chance?

So I buy a box of fortune cookies. Extracting the fortunes gives me a queasy feeling, as if I were taking out the tongues of oracles. When the cookies are empty and look as innocent as snails, I insert the neatly typed fortunes destined for them: lines from my students' poems. "The world is a dictionary of smells not easily indexed." "Even an outspoken lump has its place." "I've learned to dream in either light or dark." "What can be old that sings?"

On the last day of class, my students are startled to find that for once in their lives, their destiny comes not from the stars but from themselves. They go out into a violent world with good fortunes in their pockets: the blessings they gave each other.

Acknowledgments

Grateful acknowledgment is made to the following authors, publishers, and journals for permission to reprint previously published materials:

"What We Write about When We Write about Love," and "Put It on the Back Burner" first appeared in *The Writer;* Part 1 of "Players in the Minor League" was published in *Michigan Quarterly Review* under the title "The Writer's Ark." "The Friendship Tarot," from *Between Friends,* ed. Mickey Pearlman (Houghton Mifflin, 1994); "A Wand Made of Words: The Litany Poem," *An Exaltation of Forms,* ed. Annie Finch and Kathrine Varnes (University of Michigan Press, 2002); "The Left-Handed Story," first appeared in *Signals;* "A Tale Out of Time," first appeared in *The Horn Book;* "The Sorcerer's Apprentice: A Conversation with Harry Roseman, Assistant to Joseph Cornell," *Michigan Quarterly Review;* "Crossing the Water," *Spiritus: A Journal of Christian Spirituality* 4: 1 (2004), 78–83. © The Johns Hopkins University Press; "Not by Bread Alone: A Portrait of Simone Levy," first appeared in *Witness;* "Eden Revisited," first appeared in *The Worcester Review,* Vol. XXVI, Nox. 1&2, p. 68–69; "From the Ancestors" was first printed in *Gettysburg Review,* Volume 13, number 1 (Spring 2000), and is reprinted here with the acknowledgment of the editors;. "An Ode to the Pantry," first appeared in *Copia,* vol. 5, #1, 2002; "The Cookies of Fortune," *College English.* Copyright 1998 by the National Council of Teachers of English. Reprinted with permission; "To make a prairie, it takes a clover and one bee" and "Because I could not stop for death" by Emily Dickinson reprinted by permission of the publishers and the Trustees of Amherst College from *The Poems of Emily Dickinson,* Thomas H. Johnson, ed., Cambridge, Mass.: The Belknap Press of Harvard University Press, Copyright © 1951, 1955, 1979, 1983 by the President and Fellows of Harvard College; Excerpted material from *Complete Writings* (1965) by William Blake, edited by Geoffrey Keynes reprinted by permission of Oxford University Press; "The Killer," *Technicians of the Sacred* (University of California Press) by permission of the author/editor Jerome Rothenberg; Excerpted material from *Letters of Rainer Maria Rilke, Volume II,* translated by Jane Bannard Greene and M.D. Herter Norton, by permission of W.W. Norton & Company, Inc. Excerpted material from *Teaching Photography* (RIT Gary Graphic

Text design by Mary H. Sexton

Typesetting by Delmastype, Ann Arbor, Michigan

Text Font: Monotype Garamond
Monotype Garamond is based on roman types cut by
Jean Jannon in 1615, following the designs of Claude Garamond
which had been cut in the previous century.
It is a beautiful typeface with an air of informality
that works well for setting text.
—courtesy fonts.com